Hi there! Volume two is here with a bang. Thank you for all your support! This time, I've put my pet cat on my head. Well, not really, because it's too heavy. Anyway, there are a whole lot of strange new characters appearing in volume two. Hope you have a lot of fun with them!

—Akira Amano, 2004

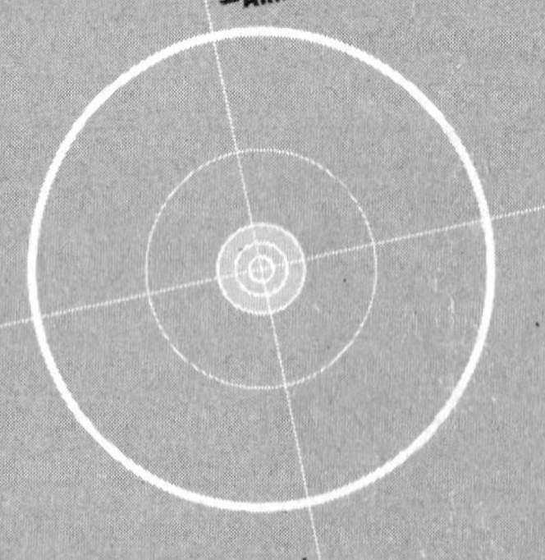

Akira Amano was born in Aichi Prefecture, located in central Japan. After early versions of the series were published in *seinen* (young men's) manga magazines, *Reborn!* first appeared in *Weekly Shonen Jump* as a stand-alone short story in late 2003. The massive success of this one-shot story led *Weekly Shonen Jump* to begin serializing *Reborn!* in mid-2004. Amano's work, with its entertaining mix of action, comedy and drama, remains extremely popular with readers.

REBORN! VOL. 2 The SHONEN JUMP ADVANCED Manga Edition

STORY AND ART BY AKIRA AMANO

Translation/JN Productions
Touch-up Art & Lettering/Freeman Wong
Design/Courtney Utt
Editor/Urian Brown

Managing Editor/Frances E. Wall
Editorial Director/Elizabeth Kawasaki
VP & Editor in Chief/Yumi Hoashi
Sr. Director of Acquisitions/Rika Inouye
Sr. VP of Marketing/Liza Coppola
Exec. VP of Sales & Marketing/John Easum
Publisher/Hyoe Narita

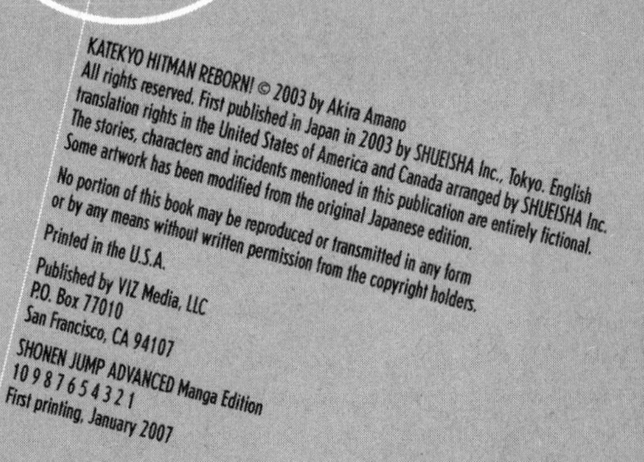

Printed in the U.S.A.

Published by VIZ Media, LLC
P.O. Box 77010
San Francisco, CA 94107

SHONEN JUMP ADVANCED Manga Edition
10 9 8 7 6 5 4 3 2 1
First printing, January 2007

www.viz.com

www.shonenjump.com

PARENTAL ADVISORY
REBORN! is rated T+ for Older Teen and is recommended for ages 16 and up. This volume contains alcohol and tobacco use and graphic, realistic violence.

SHONEN JUMP ADVANCED Manga Edition
REBORN!
Story & Art by AKIRA AMANO
2
BIANCHI

CHARACTERS

At the request of the 9th generation boss of the Vongola family, Reborn has come to Japan to teach Tsuna to become a Mafia boss. He uses the Deathperation Shot and many other means to mercilessly train Tsuna. Leon, a shape-shifting chameleon, sits atop his hat.

(AKA Tsuna) A hapless middle school student who doesn't do well in classes, isn't good at sports and isn't popular with the girls. Tsuna was languishing until he became a candidate to become the 10th generation boss of the Vongola family. Now he spends his days training to be a Mafia boss!

Tsuna's mother.

STORY THUS FAR

A tutor from Italy arrives at the home of Tsuna, a hapless middle school student. The tutor's name is Reborn, and although he looks like a baby, his occupation is—a top-flight assassin?! His mission is to make Tsuna the 10th generation boss of the Vongola crime family! Now Tsuna's life is at stake, as he learns that anything is possible if one is "deathperate."

A 7th grader who is the shining hope of the school baseball team. One of the few friends Tsuna has among his classmates. An all-around good guy.

The first member of Tsuna's "family." An expert with explosives, Hayato keeps dynamite hidden all over his body. His admiration for Tsuna goes to extremes.

Hitman from the Bovina family who is out to kill Reborn.

The girl of Tsuna's dreams.

NEW FACES

CONTENTS

BIANCHI

CONTENTS

Family Entrance Examination

YAWN... I'M SO SLEEPY.

YO, TSUNA.
YAMA-MOTO! MORNING!

WHAT'S THE MATTER-NOT ENOUGH SLEEP? YOU'VE GOT BAGS UNDER YOUR EYES.
YEAH, UH...
I KNOW.

I WANT TO STAY JUST FRIENDS WITH YAMAMOTO...
I CAN'T TELL HIM ABOUT ALL THE MAYHEM THAT HAPPENED WHEN AN ASSASSIN FROM ANOTHER GANG CRIED ON ME AFTER TRYING TO KILL THE ASSASSIN WHO'S STAYING AT MY PLACE...

WELL, AS LONG AS YOU AREN'T LOSING SLEEP BECAUSE YOU WERE STUDYING...
EH?

DON'T WANT TO LOSE ONE OF OUR SLOW GROUP, RIGHT?
AH HA HA HA

AH HA HA HA
BUMP
HUH?
HE BUMPED HIM LIKE THEY WERE BUDS!

DAMN THAT GUY!
ACTING SO CHUMMY WITH TENTH GENERATION.
CRUNCH

REBORN ...
DO YOU SERIOUSLY INTEND TO ADMIT THAT GUY INTO THE FAMILY?
I DON'T INTEND TO- HE'S ALREADY IN. I'VE DECIDED.

DOOM
WHAT?

AH HA HA HA
BUMP
OH! HE DID IT TO TENTH GENERATION AGAIN!
DAMN HIM ...!

PLEASE RECONSIDER, REBORN!
I'M ABSOLUTELY AGAINST ADMITTING SUCH A RUDE GUY!
SPLURT
HUH?
WAS HE LISTENING TO ME...?
ANYWAY, IN ORDER TO SATISFY GOKUDERA, I'VE DECIDED TO GIVE YAMAMOTO A "FAMILY ENTRANCE TEST."
FLOOOAAT
I CAN'T GO ALONG WITH THAT!
YOU DIDN'T EVEN ASK ME!
AND DON'T GO INTO THE SCHOOL POOL WITHOUT PERMISSION!
YAMAMOTO IS MY CLASSMATE! MY FRIEND!
BESIDES, HE'S BUSY WITH BASEBALL!
DON'T DRAG HIM INTO YOUR WEIRD WORLD.

I'VE ALREADY SENT GOKUDERA TO SUMMON YAMAMOTO.
SPLASH
WHAT?!
Y-YOU'RE TALKING ABOUT THAT GOKU-DERA!
WHAT IF SOME-THING HAPPENS TO YAMA-MOTO?!
DASH

DOOM

HEY, HEY GOKU-DERA...
GLARE
GLARE
YOU ASKED ME TO COME HERE, SO WHY'RE YOU GLARING AT ME ME LIKE THAT?
GLARE
GLARE
WHAT A DISGUST-ING GUY...
THERE'S NO WAY A WUSS LIKE HIM CAN PROTECT THE BOSS!

HUFF... NOTHING'S HAPPENED SO FAR... GOOD.
Pant
Pant
Pant
YO.
BOSS!
SWUFF
YOU SHOULD DRINK SOME MILK.
YOU'RE EDGY BECAUSE YOU DON'T GET ENOUGH CALCIUM.
SNAP
THAT'S IT...
SWOOSH
HEY!
!

?!
WHO'S THAT?
YOUR YOUNGER BROTHER, TSUNA?
HUH?

CIAO-SU.
UH OH.
REBORN! NO WONDER I FELT SO HEAVY...
I'M NOT HIS YOUNGER BROTHER.
I'M REBORN, AN ASSASSIN FROM THE MAFIA VONGOLA FAMILY.

OH NO! STUPID!
HE GAVE HIMSELF AWAY FROM THE VERY START!

HA HA HA HA!
THAT SO?
OH, FORGIVE ME.
HUH ?!

THAT'S PRETTY IMPRESSIVE-AN ASSASSIN SO YOUNG.
NOT REALLY.
YOU'RE GOING TO JOIN THE VONGOLA FAMILY, TOO.

NOW JUST A MINUTE, REBORN!
TAKE IT EASY, HE'S JUST A KID.

REMEMBER PLAYING AS A KID?
COPS AND ROBBERS AND THAT SORT OF STUFF.

WHAT!
HE THINKS WE'RE PLAYING MAFIA?!
DOOM

TSUNA IS THE FAMILY'S TENTH-GENERATION BOSS.
UP YOU GO.
HYOI
PLOP
ARGH!
OH... YOU MADE A VERY GOOD CHOICE.

THAT REBORN! IF I EVEN TOUCH HIM, HE NEARLY KILLS ME.
BUT IN FRONT OF YAMAMOTO, HE ACTS LIKE A GOOD LITTLE KITTEN!
GRIN

OKAY, I GOT YOU.
THEN COUNT ME IN... THAT VONGOLA FAMILY OF YOURS.
SMILE

EH?! Y... YAMA-MOTO ?!
WHAT'RE YOU SAYING ?!

TSK!

SO, WHAT DO I HAVE TO DO?
FIRST, YOU HAVE TO TAKE A FAMILY ENTRANCE TEST.

OH... A TEST, EH? THAT'S PRETTY SERIOUS.
IF YOU DON'T PASS THE TEST, WE WON'T LET YOU JOIN THE FAMILY.
BOING
AH...

TH.. THAT'S IT...
AS LONG AS HE DOESN'T PASS THE TEST, THEN...

JUST SO YOU KNOW, FAILING THE TEST MEANS YOU'LL DIE.
GASP!!
WHAT?!

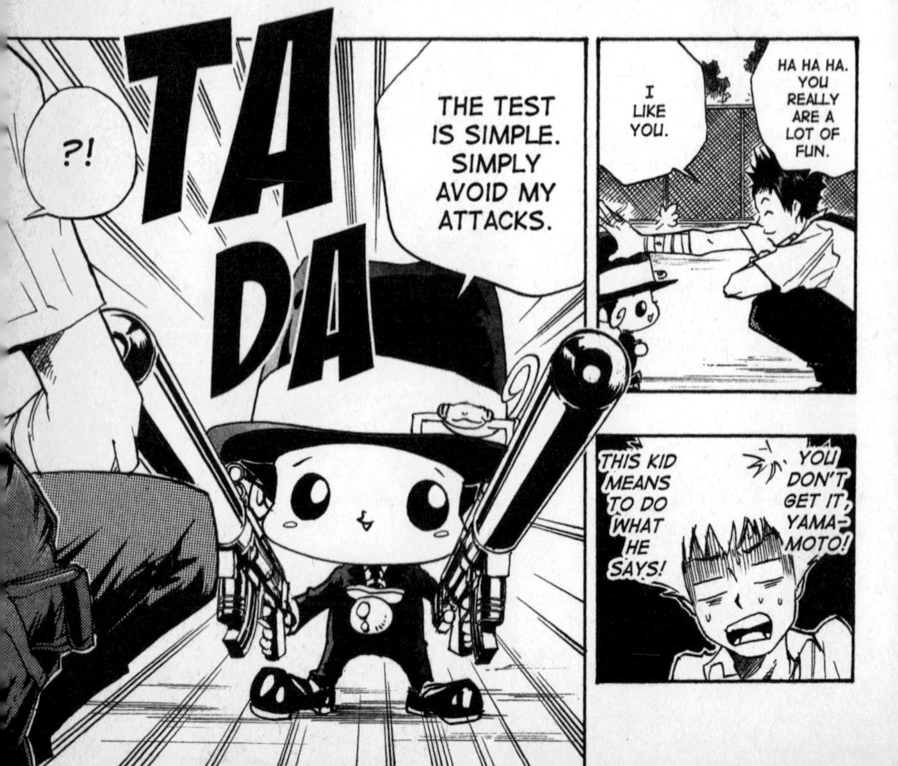
HA HA HA. YOU REALLY ARE A LOT OF FUN.
I LIKE YOU.
YOU DON'T GET IT, YAMAMOTO!
THIS KID MEANS TO DO WHAT HE SAYS!
THE TEST IS SIMPLE. SIMPLY AVOID MY ATTACKS.
TA DA
?!

OKAY, LET'S BEGIN.
WE'LL START WITH THE KNIVES.
SWFF
SWFF SWFF
SWFF
!!
VSS
WHOA!
VSS
VSS

WAIT! WAIT REBORN!
ARE YOU SERIOUSLY PLANNING TO KILL YAMAMOTO?!
ZO
OM

DIDN'T YOU PLAY WITH WOODEN SWORDS WHEN YOU WERE A KID?
COME ON, LET'S HUMOR HIM.
HUH
?!
HE STILL THINKS IT'S JUST A KID'S GAME!

KILL HIM. KILL HIM.
WAIT A SEC, TSUNA.
GRAB
EH?

AS THE BOSS, SHOW HIM HOW IT'S DONE, TSUNA.
HUH ?!
THAT'S A GREAT IDEA. WE'LL HAVE A CONTEST TO SEE WHO PASSES THE TEST.
WAIT.
HUH ?!
OKAY, RUN!
HEY... WAIT!
SPRINT
THAT WAS CLOSE.
WSHH
GAD! HIS LIFE'S AT STAKE- AND HE'S ENJOYING IT!
HIS BASEBALL TRAINING IS PAYING OFF.
HE'S GOT INCRED-IBLE REFLEXES.
HE'S GOT A GOOD ARM.
WSHH
OH, IS THAT SO...
Tsk.

TOYS NOWADAYS SURE LOOK REAL.
I'D SWEAR THOSE WERE KNIVES WERE REAL.
YOU THINK THEY'RE *TOYS* ?!
GASP!!
DOOM
THE NEXT WEAPON IS THE CROSSBOW.
AGH!
SCREECH
HE CUT US OFF!
HE'S GOOD.

GA HA HA HA HA. FOUND YOU, REBORN!

NOW WHAT?
NO... IT CAN'T BE.

I'M LAMBO FROM THE BOVINO FAMILY!
I'M ONLY FIVE, BUT I'VE COME TO JUNIOR HIGH!

I KNOW! BOSS IN ITALY ...
SHUFFLE SHUFFLE
..SENT ME A WEAPON BECAUSE I WORKED SO HARD.

DIE, REBORN!
KERCHUNK
DOOSH
DOOSH
DOOSH
WHAT THE ?!
B- B- BOOM
GYAAAA!!
FWSHH

ALMOST... JUST TEN METERS MORE.

RUMBLE
WHEW ...

REBORN! STOP THE TEST!
DIDN'T YOU SEE THAT?
LAMBO LAUNCHED ROCKETS AT US!
TOSS

IF I TAKE THESE GUYS LIGHTLY ...
...I MIGHT NOT PASS.

NEXT IS THE SUB-MACHINEGUN.
H... HEY!
CHACK

I'LL BEGIN WITH THE AIM OF AN APPRENTICE ASSASSIN.
RA TA TA TA TA
HYAAAA!!

WHOOSH WHOOSH
RA TA TA TAT
AAGH! HERE THEY COME!
SPAK
TAK
TINK

B-B-BOOM
WAAGH!!

YOU CAN BLAST AWAY, TOO, GOKUDERA.
RA TA TA TAT
!

GO AHEAD LIKE YOU'RE GOING TO KILL YAMA-MOTO.
!!

WELL, GUESS I HAVE NO CHOICE ...
IF REBORN SAYS SO...
GRR GRR

BOSS!
?!

MOVE ASIDE.
WINK
OKAY?
SHAKE SHAKE

HUH?

DARN YOU, REBORN!
CLICK
THIS CALLS FOR THE TEN-YEAR BAZOOKA.

BOOM

OH WELL ...
PLUME
I GUESS IT'S UP TO LAMBO FROM TEN YEARS IN THE FUTURE.
FOR THE FINALE: ROCKETS.
CLICK
YOU'LL SEE...
PLUME
PLUME
PLUME
THUN-DER.
SET.
SPARK

WHOOOSH
FWSH
FWSH
FWSH
DZOOM
BZAA
HEY, HEY...
G- G- G- GAGH !!
KABOOM
GYAAAA!!

MAYBE I GOT CARRIED AWAY ...
UH OH ...
ARE YOU ALL RIGHT, BOSS?
BOSS!!
HE'S OVER THERE.
!
BAM
WHEW... THAT WAS REALLY CLOSE.
I'M STILL ALIVE ...
...BECAUSE YAMAMOTO PULLED ME OUT.

YOU PASSED THE TEST. YOU'RE OFFICIALLY ONE OF THE FAMILY.
THANK YOU.

GRAB
FUME FUME

YOU DID GOOD.
!

YOU CAN BE HIS EARLOBES.
BUT I HAVE NO INTENTION OF GIVING UP MY POSITION AS TSUNA'S RIGHT-HAND MAN.

YOU PROTECTED THE BOSS. I'LL HAVE TO ACCEPT YOU AS ONE OF THE FAMILY.
BUT REMEMBER, I'M HIS RIGHT-HAND MAN.
YOU'RE JUST HIS COLLAR-BONE.
C... COLLAR-BONE?!

GA HA
HA HA HA
I ALWAYS THOUGHT YOU WERE A FUNNY GUY, GOKUDERA!

IN A WAY, MAYBE THOSE TWO GET ALONG?
DOOOM
WHAT?
WHAT'D YOU JUST SAY?! YOU'RE HIS NOSE HAIRS!
UGH.
THEN YOU'RE HIS BOOGER!

GUYS?!

HE STILL THINKS THAT WAS JUST A GAME OF MAFIA!
THOSE EXPLOSIONS JUST NOW-TOYS THESE DAYS ARE SO REALISTIC...
DOOOM

WELL, I'M OFF TO PRACTICE.
SEE YOU LATER, KID.
YEAH.

THEY'RE BOTH SET ON BEING MY MEN!
STOP IT!

OOOOOOO

...

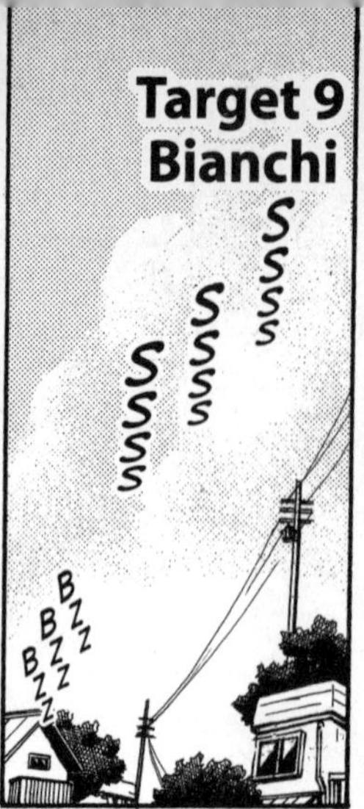
Target 9
Bianchi
SSSS
SSSS
SSSS
BZZ
BZZ
BZZ

MAN, IS IT HOT.
BZZ
I SURE COULD USE A DRINK.
BZZ
BZZ

RING RING

RING
RING
ULP

A HELMET AND GOGGLES... ON A SHOPPING BICYCLE?

SCREEECH
TAP

SSSU...

Target 9
Bianchi

OW!
BONK
MUFF
RING
RING
SODA

PSHEW—
TONK
SODA

AW, IT SPILLED ...
NOW THAT REALLY SUCKED ...!

?!
BSHWAA

WHAT THE HECK'S HAPPEN-ING?!
WHIZZ
SHWAA
FAP

GAWK!
HUH?

REBORN, WE'VE GOT TROUBLE!
OUT-SIDE!
JUICE!
A BIRD!
HUH?
GYAAA!!
YECK!!
DO YOU EXUDE SAP OR SOME-THING?!
THEY'RE MY SUMMER HENCHMEN.
THEY COLLECT INFORMATION FOR ME.
BUZZ
BUZZ
BUZZ
BUZZ
ARE YOU TELLING ME YOU SPEAK INSECT?!
THANKS TO THEM, I HAVE INFORMA-TION...
THAT BIANCHI IS IN TOWN.
BIANCHI...? WHO'S THAT?
AN ASSASSIN FRIEND OF MINE FROM WAY BACK.

WHAT?
DING DONG
Italian pizza delivery.
!
TOMP
TOMP
TOMP
PIZZA?
MOM, ARE YOU HOME?

THANK YOU FOR WAITING.
I'VE COME WITH YOUR VONGOLE PIZZA ORDER.
PIZZA
Y...
YOU'RE THAT WOMAN I JUST MET!

SNAP

BSHUU
?!
ENJOY!

UGH!
I... CAN'T BREATHE ...!

PSHUUU

WIZZ
WIZZ
WIZZ
FAP
FAP
FAP
PLOP
CIAO-SU, BIANCHI.
SNAP
REBORN.
PIZZA
HUH?
SO WHY AM I...
...ABOUT TO BE KILLED?
CHOKE CHOKE
SHE'S BIANCHI ?!
I'VE COME FOR YOU.
LET'S WORK BIG HITS TOGETHER AGAIN, REBORN.
HUH ?!

YOU DON'T FIT IN WITH PEACE-FUL PLACES.
YOU BELONG IN THE MORE DANGER-OUS AND THRILLING UNDER-WORLD.
RA TA TA TA TA TA
PSHU
RA TA

I MADE IT CLEAR, BIANCHI.
I HAVE A JOB TO DO TRAINING TSUNA. I CAN'T GO WITH YOU.

...
...POOR DEAR REBORN.
SOB
HUH?

UNLESS THIS TENTH GENERATION DIES OF SOME UNFORTUNATE ACCIDENT, REBORN...
...YOU WON'T EVER BE FREE, WILL YOU?
SOB
IS THAT WHY YOU TRIED TO KILL ME?!
YOU'RE CRAZY!
WHAT ?!
DOOM
ANY-WAY, I'LL BE GOING.
WHEN I KILL ...
....THE TENTH GENERATION, I'LL COME FOR YOU AGAIN.
HEY...
WHAT THE HECK ARE YOU TALKING ABOUT ?!

WHO THE HECK IS THAT WOMAN ?!
SHE'S A FREELANCE ASSASSIN CALLED POISON SCORPION BIANCHI.
HER SPECIAL KILLING TECHNIQUE IS TO MAKE HER VICTIMS EAT HER POISON COOKING.

ANOTHER WEIRDO!
WHAT'S GOING ON IN YOUR LINE OF WORK, ANY-WAY?!
IT LOOKED LIKE SHE HAD A THING FOR YOU.
BIANCHI IS MADLY IN LOVE WITH ME.
WE WERE EVEN DATING FOR A WHILE.

HUH ?!

D...DATING? YOU MEAN SHE WAS YOUR GIRL FRIEND ...?!
I'M VERY POPULAR, YOU KNOW.

BIANCHI IS MY WOMAN.
DA-DOOM
NO.4
DO YOU UNDER-STAND WHAT YOU'RE SAYING ?!

ANY-HOW... DO SOME-THING!
SHE'S AFTER MY LIFE!
TSUNA... ALL HUMAN BEINGS DIE SOMEDAY.
SIP SIP
TEA
DON'T GET PHILOSO-PHICAL ALL OF A SUDDEN!
CHIRP CHIRP CHIRP
MORNING, TSUNA-KUN.
!
MORNING, KYOKO!
WHAT A GREAT WAY TO START THE MORNING.
TODAY, WE'RE LEARNING HOW TO MAKE RICEBALLS IN HOME ECONOMICS.
It'll be fun!
YEAH.
RING RING
UH-OH!
?
RING RING
I'LL SEND ANYONE WHO GETS IN THE WAY OF THE MAN I LOVE...
...TO HIS DEATH SMOTHERED IN POISON!

HERE.
!
TOSS
TOSS
SODA
NO!
CLANG
DO YOU KNOW THAT PERSON, TSUNA?
N... NO... I WONDER WHO SHE WAS?
THAT BIANCHI...
DOES SHE INTEND TO INVOLVE KYOKO, TOO?
WHIZZ
WHIZZ
FAP
FAP
SODA
SODA
DING DONG

TODAY, WE'RE GIVING AWAY THE RICEBALLS WE MADE IN HOME ECONOMICS CLASS...
TA-DA
JUST FOR YOU GUYS!
YEAH!
YAY

WHAT A STRANGE EVENT.
TSUNA, HAVE YOU DECIDED WHOSE YOU WANT?
HUH?
THAT'S... OBVIOUS ...

I WANT KYOKO'S RICEBALL, BUT...

GASP
!!
THAT'S!
BIANCHI!

BSHWAA
WHAT THE ...?!
SHE SWITCHED KYOKO'S RICE-BALLS?!
HOLD IT.
WHAT'D YOU JUST DO?!

?!
HUH? WHERE'D SHE GO?
TSUNA-KUN.
WANT ONE?
DOOM
GONG
EH ?!
YOU'RE REALLY GOING FOR IT, AREN'T YOU!
BUMP
UH...
KYAA KYAA KYAA
NO... I UH ...
BSHWAA
I'M SUPPOSED TO EAT THIS?!
UH...
SHnn
YOU DON'T LIKE SALMON?
!
NO, IT'S NOT THAT AT ALL...
DON'T LOOK AT ME LIKE THAT, KYOKO!

BUT IF I EAT IT, I'LL DIE.
HAA HAA
WHAT CAN I DO?

HAA HAA

I'VE ALWAYS BELIEVED A PERSON WOULD DIE FOR THE ONE THEY LOVE.
SO, DIE FOR LOVE, TENTH GENERA-TION OF THE VONGOLA FAMILY.

IF YOU WON'T EAT IT, BOSS, WE'LL TAKE THEM.
!
GOOD IDEA, GOKU-DERA.

WAIT.
I'LL TAKE ONE.
HELP YOUR-SELF.
AAGHHH
!!

YOU'LL DIE IF YOU EAT THOSE!
WHACK
WHACK
!
TSUNA?
SPARKLE
YOU DID A GOOD JOB PROTECTING YOUR FAMILY.
GRIN
JUST AS THEIR BOSS SHOULD.
BANG

I'LL EAT THOSE RICEBALLS WITH DEATHPER-ATION!
RIP
MO KK
GOBBLE GOBBLE
MGG
MGG MGG
DELICIOUS!
GULP

!!
MY POISON COOKING HAS NO EFFECT!
A DEATHPER-ATION SHOT TO HIS BELLY BUTTON GIVES HIM AN IRON STOMACH.
NOTHING HE EATS WILL AFFECT HIM.

MORE!
SWIPE
SWIPE
SWIPE
SWIPE
SWIPE
HUH? MY RICE-BALLS, THEY'RE ...
LOOK!
TSUNA'S EATING THEM!
MSHA
MSHA
STILL NOT ENOUGH!
GYAAA
WOW! HE'S EATING EVERY-THING IN SIGHT!
SOME-BODY STOP HIM!
HE'S LOST IT.
UGH
WAAA
...

CURSE THE VONGOLA TENTH GENERATION.
BUT I SWEAR I'LL MAKE REBORN MINE SOMEDAY.
REBORN WAS OBLIVIOUS TO BIANCHI'S FEELINGS.
OH, A HERCULES BEETLE.

THE RICEBALL INCIDENT HAD UNEXPECTED REPERCUSSIONS.
THAT COULDN'T BE...
NO, I'M SURE OF IT.

YOU CAN TAKE THAT AS SAWADA'S DECLARATION OF LOVE.
HUH?!
THAT WAS A MANLY THING TO DO, BOSS.
I'LL KILL ANYONE WHO EATS...
...THE RICEBALLS KYOKO GAVE ME, YOU HEAR!
WAY TO GO, TSUNA.
EVERYONE TOOK TSUNA'S "YOU'LL DIE IF YOU EAT THOSE!"...
JUST WHAT I'D EXPECT FROM YOU, TENTH GENERATION.
...IN A DIFFERENT WAY.

Give us back our riceballs...
GG GG GG GG GG
HYEE

Target 10
Poison Cooking II

BZZ BZZ
PHEW... IS IT EVER HOT!
I THINK I'LL JUST TURN ON THE AC AND CHILL IN MY ROOM.
GCHA
THUNK
?
NYUM...
HE'S SO TIRED FROM TRYING TO KILL PEOPLE THAT HE WENT BEDDY-BYE.
!
CIAO-SU.
RING
YOU SURE ARE ENJOYING JAPAN'S SUMMER TO THE FULLEST!
ROLL ROLL
FESTIVAL

I HAVE SOME FOR YOU, TOO.
!
EAT UP.
BSHWA
BIANCHI!!
BSHWAA
WHAT ...
WHAT'RE YOU DOING HERE?!
FLOP
WITH THAT DEADLY-LOOKING DISH!
I'M HERE FOR LOVE.
SHE'S HERE TO DO A JOB.
REBORN CAN'T DO ANYTHING WITHOUT ME.
I WAS THINKING OF HAVING BIANCHI HANDLE SOME OF YOUR TUTORING DUTIES.
HOW DIFFERENT CAN THEY GET?!

WHAT'RE YOU TALKING ABOUT, YOU MAKING HER MY TUTOR OUT OF THE BLUE?! YOU'VE HARDLY DONE ANYTHING YOURSELF!
BESIDES, THAT WOMAN'S TRYING TO KILL ME WITH HER POISON COOKING!
OH HO... YOU'RE STILL SUCH A CHILD.
HOW LONG ARE YOU GOING TO LET THAT WORRY YOU?
HUH?

RIGHT NOW, I'M DEVELOPING POISON COOKING II.
WITH TWO TIMES THE KILLING POWER.
ALL THE MORE REASON I WANT YOU OUT OF HERE!

KCHA
I'LL BE HANDLING HOME ECONOMICS AND FINE ARTS.
TODAY, WE'LL BE DO A HOME ECONOMICS EXERCISE. I'LL BE IN THE KITCHEN GETTING THINGS READY.
JUST A MINUTE.
IT'S ONLY JUST A MATTER OF TIME BEFORE I'M KILLED!
DOOM

DING DONG
BOSS!
UGH... THAT VOICE... NOT NOW...!
STOP SLURP-ING...
SLURP
CHASE HER OUT!
REBORN, DO SOME-THING!
G... GOKUDERA, WHAT BRINGS YOU HERE?
TUP
TUP
TUP
WANT TO SHARE THIS MELON? I'M TOLD IT'S REALLY SWEET.
SMILE
BREAK
I REALLY APPRECIATE THAT, BUT NOW'S REALLY NOT THE BEST TIME...
AND THAT'S NO LIE...
GLA RE
!

YOU'VE GOT TROUBLE, DON'T YOU?
THEN I'LL TAKE CARE OF IT.
HUH ?!

I SUPPOSE YOU COULD CALL IT TROUBLE, BUT...
AH!

BUT GOKUDERA JUST MIGHT BE ABLE...
...TO CHASE BIANCHI AWAY.
GET LOST!
RAWR
SOB SOB

ACTUALLY, THERE'S SOME-ONE HERE...
SPLAT

OH NO, THE WATER-MELON!

BIG SIS!
DROP

HUH?
HAYATO.

HUH?
SISTER?
WHAT?
GROWL
HGAAH
THUD
DA
EXCUSE ME!
SH

WAIT!
D-D-D-DASH
GOKU-DERA?!

HE ALWAYS DOES THAT.
STRANGE KID.
BIG... SISTER...?
THAT MEANS... SHE'S ...

HUH?!
YOU MEAN GOKUDERA AND BIANCHI ARE SIBLINGS?!
YUP. BUT WITH DIFFERENT MOTHERS.

THERE YOU ARE!
GOKU-DERA...
WHEEZE WHEEZE
PANT PANT

I...UH... I'M SORRY ABOUT WHAT HAPPENED...
...TO THE WATER-MELON YOU BROUGHT.
I'M... AFRAID ...

BIG SIS AND I LIVED WITH EACH OTHER UNTIL I WAS EIGHT.
WHEEZE
?!

WE HELD MANY GRANDIOSE PARTIES AT OUR MANSION.
WHEN I TURNED SIX, I WAS TO PERFORM A PIANO RECITAL IN FRONT OF EVERYONE FOR THE FIRST TIME.

M... MANSION ?!
GOKUDERA'S ACTUALLY FROM A VERY RICH FAMILY?!

THAT WAS WHEN SIS BAKED HER FIRST BATCH OF COOKIES FOR ME..
I BAKED THESE JUST FOR YOU, HAYATO.
ENJOY.
THANK YOU.

THAT WAS HER FIRST POISON COOKING DISH...
BSHWAA

LATER, I LEARNED THAT SIS HAD A TALENT FOR TURNING EVERYTHING SHE MADE INTO POISON COOKING.
WHAT'S WITH THAT ?!
SO NATURALLY, AFTER I ATE HER COOKIES, I HAD TERRIBLE DIZZY SPELLS AND ATTACKS OF NAUSEA.
MY PIANO RECITAL SOUNDED LIKE SOMETHING FROM ANOTHER WORLD....
BLECH
HUFF
BLARGY
HUFF
DOOM

BUT THAT WAS JUST THE START OF IT.
THAT CRAZY RECITAL EARNED HIGH PRAISE.
BRAVO!
AVANT-GARDE!
WONDER-FUL!
BLERG
BLUGG
WHAT?
DOOM
DAD SAID THE PERFORMACE WAS INSPIRED BY SIS'S COOKIES.
ANOTHER GOOD-LUCK COOKIE FOR OUR LITTLE MOZART?
HEH.
WHAT?
DOOM

THAT FEAR BECAME SO INGRAINED THAT NOW I GET A BELLYACHE AT THE MERE SIGHT OF SIS...
TRAGIC!
I SORT OF GOT THAT IMPRESSION- SHE'S QUITE A FORCEFUL SISTER.
YEAH, AND I CAN'T STAND HER!
...

I CAN'T GO NEAR SIS.
BOSS... ISN'T THERE A WAY YOU COULD DRIVE SIS OUT OF TOWN?
HUH ?!

W...WELL, IT'D MAKE ME REALLY HAPPY IF BIANCHI WEREN'T AROUND, TOO, BUT...
BUT... I'M NOT SURE I COULD ...
I HAVE A PLAN!
BEFORE SHE FELL IN LOVE WITH REBORN, THERE WAS A MAN SIS WAS CRAZY ABOUT.
HE DIED IN AN ACCIDENT, BUT SIS STILL HASN'T FOR-GOTTEN ABOUT HIM.

SO, WE HAVE TO FIND SOMEONE WHO LOOKS EXACTLY LIKE HER OLD BOY-FRIEND.
IF SIS SEES HIM, SHE'LL FOLLOW HIM TO THE ENDS OF THIS EARTH.
THAT'S ONE HECK OF A CRAZY PLAN!
GOKUDERA... YOUR PLAN IS IMPOSSIBLE... WHERE ARE WE GOING TO FIND AN EXACT LOOKALIKE...?
THIS IS A PICTURE OF HER OLD BOY-FRIEND.
!

I'VE SEEN THIS COW-BOY BEFORE!

VWIP

KCHA
THERE HE IS...

THE LOOK-ALIKE ONLY NEEDS TO SHOW FOR A MOMENT.
SIS WILL PROBABLY GO OFF LOOKING FOR HIM.
LAMBO, GET UP!
HUH?

SORRY TO ASK, BUT COULD YOU SUMMON YOURSELF FROM TEN YEARS IN THE FUTURE WITH YOUR TEN-YEAR BAZOOKA?
!
GULP

I... I'VE ...
...NEVER SHOT THE TEN YEAR BAZOOKA BEFORE!

HUH ?!

BOSS TOLD ME NOT TO USE THE TEN-YEAR BAZOOKA.
SWISH
WHY WOULD I EVER USE IT?
SWISH
SWISH
THIS KID IS A FIBBER!
I'M GOING TO SLEEP. GO AWAY.
SLUMP
THIS IS MY ROOM, YOU KNOW!
!
LAMBO USES THE TEN-YEAR BAZOOKA WHEN HE GETS SMASHED BY REBORN...
IF THAT'S THE CASE...
THERE HE IS!
WHOA... NOW HE'S BATHING IN THE WATER...
WIPE
WIPE
REBORN, I NEED A FAVOR.
I WANT YOU WHACK LAMBO AROUND A BIT.
NOPE.
NYUM

I THOUGHT I TOLD YOU.
SPARKLE
I DON'T MINGLE WITH THE LOWER ECHELON.
GA HA HA HA HA. YOU WON'T BE SAYING THAT MUCH LONGER, REBORN.
I, LAMBO, AM ABOUT TO COURAGEOUSLY JUMP DOWN FROM THE SECOND FLOOR!
HE'S SO SET IN HIS WAYS!
HE CAME ANYWAY ...
LUCKY

BZ
DIE, REBORN!
JUMP
CRACKLE CRACKLE CRACKLE CRACKLE CRACKLE
AA
I'LL ZAP YOU TO DEATH WITH THE STUN GUN BOSS SENT ME!
ZAPPP
ARGHH!!
AAPPP
UH OH ...
THIS IS BEYOND STUPID.
WIPE WIPE
BREAK

UH...
UWAAGH
CLICK
BOOM
SSS SSS SSS SSS SSS
JEEZ...
WHY AM I SOAKING IN WATER?
SSS SSS SSS SSS SSS
AH!
HE'S HERE! THE ADULT LAMBO!
BIANCHI, COME HERE A SEC...!
PLUME PLUME
COME HERE!
CHECK THIS OUT!

I DON'T LIKE THE IDEA OF FORCING YOU, BUT IT'S TIME WE GOT STARTED WITH OUR LESSON.
ROMEO!
!
?
DASH
ROMEO!
YOU'RE ALIVE!
GOOD!
SHE THINKS HE'S FOR REAL!
ROMEO!!
D-D-DASH
?

POISON COOKING!
SP
LAT
WHAT ?!
SPLASH
BIANCHI AND HER OLD BOYFRIEND WERE ON TERRIBLE TERMS JUST BEFORE THEY BROKE UP.
SHE'D OFTEN GET VERY ANGRY JUST THINKING ABOUT HIM.
HUH ?!
PER... SE... VER... ANCE...

YIKES
CLONK
LAMBO! GET A HOLD OF YOURSELF! DON'T FALL ASLEEP! CRY FOR ME!
MEDICAL TREATMENT FROM TEN YEARS IN THE FUTURE MIGHT BE ABLE TO SAVE HIM.
HMPH

CHIRP CHIRP
IS THAT SO...
OH.

NOW THAT YOU MENTION IT...
I HEARD HER FORMER BOYFRIEND DIED OF FOOD POISONING.

HEY
...

CHILL

MEAN-WHILE, JUST A WORD FROM REBORN...
I WISH I HAD SOME TASTY BROILED EELS TO BEAT THE SUMMER HEAT...

WAS ALL IT TOOK...
RING RING
TO SEND BIANCHI OFF TO HAMANAKO LAKE TO GET EELS.

Target 11 Haru Miura
THAT BABY BOY STROLLS BY MY FENCE EVERY MORNING.

HIS NAME IS REBORN. WHAT A CUTE NAME.

I WANT TO SQUEEEEZE HIM...
SIGH
...AND GIVE HIM A GREAT BIG HUG.
DRIP DRIP

Target 11 Haru Miura

BZZ
BZZ
HE'S COMING!
IF I'M GOING TO DECLARE MY LOVE, I'VE GOT TO GET ON HIS LEVEL!
GRAB
EXCUSE ME.
UPSY...
OOPSY...
SHAKE
SHAKE
TREMBLE
TREMBLE
WHAT ...?!
BLINK
WHAT'S THAT ?!
BOP
HI...
CIAO-SU.

MY NAME IS... HARU MIURA.
I KNOW. YOU LIVE HERE, RIGHT?

HE SAYS HE KNOWS ABOUT ME!
WOULD YOU BE MY FRIEND?
BLUSH
BLUSH

SURE.
AAHH ...
TOPPLE
AH!
HEY ...

YA.
PLOP

I DID IT!
SO WEIRD ...

I UH...
THMP THMP THMP
I KNOW THIS IS OUT OF THE BLUE, BUT...
THMP
...WOULD YOU...
LET ME GIVE YOU A BIG HUG?
WHAT'S THAT ABOUT ...?
DON'T GET TOO CLOSE.
GASP
HUH?
I'M AM AN ASSASSIN, YOU KNOW.
CH
CK
HEY, REBORN ...
DON'T SAY THAT IN BROAD DAY-LIGHT ...
WHACK
HUH?

YOU'RE THE LOWEST!
WHAT A THING TO TEACH HIM! ...KILL-ING?

HUH ?!
FUME FUME
BABIES ARE ANGELS WITH HEARTS OF PRISTINE WHITE!
YOU WOULD DESTROY THAT HELPLESS INNOCENCE WITH YOUR ROTTEN HEART?!
WOULD YOU ?!
NNGH
GRAB
WHAT'S THIS GIRL TALKING ABOUT?
YOU'VE GOT IT ALL WRONG ...
THIS IS A MISUNDER-STANDING!
IN WHAT WAY?
I DIDN'T TEACH REBORN ABOUT KILLING!

YOU'RE A LIAR!
YOU'RE REBORN'S OLDER BROTHER, AREN'T YOU? I'VE SEEN YOU TOGETHER MANY TIMES!
WE'RE NOT BROTHERS!
THEN THAT MAKES YOU EVEN WORSE!
YOU'RE TURNING SOMEONE ELSE'S BABY INTO A DEVIL!
I'M NOT GETTING THROUGH.

HEAR ME? YOU'D BETTER NOT GO NEAR REBORN AGAIN!
ZWI
YOU'RE A BAD INFLUENCE.
SHE'S RIGHT IN MY FACE!
I'M AFRAID NOT.

HUH?
THAT'S RIGHT. YOU EXPLAIN IT TO HER.
WHY SHOULD I BE THE ONE WHO GETS HIT?

IT'S MY JOB TO TRAIN TSUNA TO BE TENTH GENERATION BOSS OF THE MAFIA.
I CAN'T LEAVE TSUNA'S SIDE UNTIL THEN.
S
!
SLUG
THE MAFIA?! I'VE HAD ENOUGH OF THIS CRAZY ACT!
YOU'VE EVEN TAKEN REBORN'S FREEDOM AWAY!
GASP
I'VE... BEEN PUNCHED BY A GIRL'S FIST!
HUGGING REBORN WILL HAVE TO COME LATER!
I HAVE TO PROTECT HIM FIRST.

WAIT ...
JUST A MINUTE!
!
RRROAAR
I THINK SHE HATES ME...
LATER.
WHAT'S WITH THIS GIRL?

YOU TWO ARE A PERFECT MATCH.
JUST LIKE A MARRIED COUPLE.
YEAH-- ON THE VERGE OF A DIVORCE!

SAWADA

POOR LITTLE REBORN ...
THAT BOY CONTROLS HIM.
PEEK

WAIT FOR ME, LITTLE REBORN ...
HARU WILL FREE YOU.

SEEMS YOU TWO GET ALONG.
GR
AB
?
WHA?!
FLAIL FLAIL
DRAAAG
POISON SAKE

YAY!
SO YOU WANT TO SAVE REBORN, TOO?

HE'S CUTE, ISN'T HE?
YES, HE'S WONDER-FUL.

BUT THAT TSUNA'S TRYING TO FORCE REBORN TO PLAY ASSASSIN.
GLMP GLMP
REBORN IS THE BEST ASSASSIN THERE IS.
!

OH COME ON, WHAT'RE YOU TALKING ABOUT?
GLMP
AHH... I'LL NEVER FORGET THOSE THRILLING HITS WHEN I TEAMED WITH REBORN...

YOU'RE KIDDING!
HUH?

SHE'S... CRYING!

EVERY-THING YOU SAID ...
IS IT ALL TRUE?

READ THIS WAY

CHLANK
CHLANK
WOW IT'S HOT ...

CHLANK
CHLANK
HUH...
IT'S SO HOT, I'M STARTING TO HEAR THINGS.

CHLANK
CHLANK
IT'S NOT MY HEAR-ING?

CHLANK
GOOD MORNING.
WHO ARE YOU ...?!
CHLANK

IT'S ME, HARU. MY HEAD WAS SPINNING LAST NIGHT AND I DIDN'T GET MUCH SLEEP.
IS THAT HOW YOU DRESS WHEN YOU DON'T GET ENOUGH SLEEP?
WOBBLE

NO.
THAT WOULD MAKE ME AN IDIOT.

IF REBORN REALLY IS AN ASSASSIN ...
...AND YOU'RE GOING TO BE THE MAFIA'S TENTH-GENERATION BOSS, YOU SHOULD BE VERY STRONG.
WHAT ?!
SMUSH
IF YOU ARE INDEED STRONG, THEN I WILL BELIEVE WHAT REBORN SAID.
I WON'T COMPLAIN ABOUT REBORN'S WAY OF LIFE.

FIGHT ME!
GWAHH
WHAT THE?!
SMASH
BLADE!
WAIT ...
WAGH ...
...A MINUTE!

TENTH GENERATION?!
WAGH
BUZZ
STICK!
BLADE!
WHAT THE BLAZES IS THAT?!
WHERE'D THAT ROGUE BULLET COME FROM?!
ZIP
SHEESH!!
I'M NOT GOING TO BECOME ...
...A MAFIA BOSS!
THEN YOU WERE TAKING ADVANTAGE OF LITTLE REBORN, AFTER ALL!
THAT'S NOT HOW IT IS!

STAND BACK, BOSS!
HUH?
ZA
GET LOST!
FLING
G... GOKU-DERA!
SZZ SZZ SZZ
HUH?
THOSE...
...GO BOOM...
HUH?
BOOM?
WHOAH!
BOOM

SPLASH

OH NO, SHE FELL IN!
PHUUU
YOU'RE SAFE NOW.

GLUB BLUB
WHY'RE YOU CARRYING THINGS LIKE THAT?

!
SPLISH
THE ARMOR'S TOO HEAVY- I CAN'T SWIM!

HELP... COUGH.
SPLASH
HELP!
SPLASH

REBORN!

SHE... SHE'S IN TROUBLE!
HUH?
I'LL SAVE HER.

DON'T!
THIS RIVER IS TOO STRONG FOR YOU TO SWIM, REBORN ...
!

REBORN?
SPLASH
WHAT ARE YOU DOING?
BANG
HYUUU
WHAAAA?!
RIP
I WILL RESCUE HARU WITH DEATHPER-ATION!
DOOM
SPLISH
AHHH !?

AND FOR GOOD MEASURE.
BANG
BANG
BSS
BSS
SPIN SPIN SPIN
SHOTS TO THE HEELS CREATE FOOT PROPELLERS.
PLUNGE
HOLD ON...
SCOOP
...TO ME!
GRIN

THANK YOU VERY MUCH.
ARE YOU SORRY AT ALL?
IF ANYTHING HAD HAPPENED TO THE BOSS...
YOU WOULDN'T BE AROUND HERE NOW.

...
HUMPH!

?!

I WILL RESCUE HARU WITH DEATHPERATION!
WHISH
HOLD ON TO ME!
FSSHH
!

I THOUGHT LINES LIKE THAT...
ONLY CAME OUT ON TV.

NNGH
SHE'S NOT SORRY AT ALL!

I'LL SWIM YOU OVER TO THE FAR BANK!
HEY...
CUT THAT OUT!
YOU'RE EMBARRASSING ME!

YOU WERE SO... WONDERFUL.
YOU JUMPED IN TO SAVE ME IN REBORN'S PLACE, TENTH GENERATION?! ♡

WHAT ?!
GRIN

MY HEART'S BEEN POUNDING...
...SO MADLY, I...
HUH ?!
WAIT!
I THINK I'M IN LOVE WITH YOU, TSUNA.
YOU WHAT ?!
WHAT'S WITH THIS CRAZY GIRL...?
BUT WEREN'T YOU IN LOVE WITH REBORN?
RIGHT NOW, I WANT YOU TO GIVE ME A BIG HUG, TSUNA.
WHAT ?!
Wh... Why me ?!?
Please !!

SNEEZE
I have your towel...

Target 12 Problem 7

BZZ
BZZ

1-A
SIGH.

IT'S SUMMER BREAK ...
BUT I'VE HAD NOTHING BUT MAKE-UP CLASSES BECAUSE MY GRADES WERE SO BAD.
MATH

KYOKO'S NOT HERE, SO THIS IS TOO BORING...
THIS HANDOUT IS YOUR HOMEWORK DUE TOMORROW.
YOU MUST ANSWER EVERY QUESTION CORRECTLY, OR FAIL.
!

WHAT?!
WHAT DO YOU MEAN, "WHAT?"
NORMALLY, THAT'S HOW IT WOULD BE, BUT...
BUT THERE'S NO STRENGTH IN SMALL NUMBERS.
ALL RIGHT, THAT WILL BE ALL.
EMPTY
What?
What?
What?
MATH

WHAT'S WITH THIS CLASS? REMEDIAL CLASSES AND NOW HOMEWORK- I CAN'T GOOF OFF TODAY...
TSUNA.
SIGH
!

WANNA WORK ON THE HOMEWORK TOGETHER?
TWO WORK FASTER THAN ONE, RIGHT?
!
THAT'S A GREAT IDEA!
I'M GLAD YAMAMOTO'S ONE OF MY REMEDIAL CLASS BUDDIES.
WHERE SHALL WE WORK?
WHY NOT AT OUR PLACE?
HUHH
STOP POPPING IN AND OUT OF THE CLASS-ROOMS!
CIAO-SU.
YO KID... YOU'RE LOOKING GOOD.
I MEAN, WHY DO YOU GET TO DECIDE WHERE WE DO OUR HOME-WORK?
BECAUSE I'M YOUR TUTOR.

H... HEY!
...
HA HA HA HA
I SEE.
LIFT
TSUNA, YOU SURE GOT YOURSELF A GREAT TUTOR.
YAMAMOTO STILL THINKS IT'S A JOKE.
CAN YOU CHECK MY HOMEWORK, TOO? I'LL GIVE YOU CANDY.
HA HA HA
TA-DAH
SURE.
WHAT?!
BUT IT WON'T DO BOTH OF YOU ANY GOOD IF I MAKE IT TOO EASY.
I WON'T SAY ANYTHING UNTIL YOU GET THE HANG OF IT.

YOU'RE GOOD!
HA HA HA
PSSSU
I LIKE THIS GUY.
WAIT...
ARE YOU SERIOUS ABOUT DOING IT AT MY PLACE?!
SAWADA

LISTEN! PLEASE, BEHAVE YOURSELF, OKAY!
I TOLD YOU— I WON'T INTERFERE.
DING DONG
COMING!
HERE WE ARE!
WHY!
WHY'RE YOU HERE, GOKU-DERA?!

WHEN YOU THINK ABOUT IT, WE'LL NEVER FINISH UNLESS WE HAVE SOMEBODY WHO KNOWS THE SUBJECT.
WITH GOKUDERA HERE, WE HAVE THE STRENGTH OF MILLIONS.
CUT IT OUT.
BLUSH
G... GOKU-DERA'S A SCARY GUY...
BUT HE'S GOOD AT HIS STUDIES.
WITH GOKU-DERA'S HELP,
WE JUST MIGHT FINISH QUICKLY!

SO WITH THAT, IT COMES LIKE THIS.
GOKU-DERA, ALL YOU'VE BEEN DOING ...
...IS READING FROM THE TEXTBOOK.
WHAT ?!

LOOK YOU, IF YOU MOCK ME, I'LL KILL YOU!
THUMP
WHA...
THE SOLU-TIONS ARE ALL HERE!
I SEE, I SEE. THAT'S RIGHT.

THANKS TO YOU, I THINK I'VE JUST ABOUT FIGURED IT OUT.
SNATCH
LET ME SEE THAT!
EH?

...
TSK
MUMBLE
IT'S RIGHT.

WAY TO GO, YAMA-MOTO...
YOUR SCORES ARE LOW ONLY BECAUSE YOU'RE SO BUSY WITH BASEBALL. YOU CAN DO IT IF YOU TRY!

BUT I DON'T GET PROBLEM SEVEN AT ALL.
!
GA HA HA!
YOU'RE STILL STUPID, AFTER ALL, YAMA-MOTO!
HE HE HE
...GOKU-DERA ...

THE ANSWER TO PROBLEM SEVEN IS...
...
...I DON'T KNOW ...
EH ?!
THAT SUCKS ...
AREN'T WE GOING TO FAIL IF WE CAN'T SOLVE THEM ALL?
WH... WHAT ?!
SLAM
WHY DIDN'T YOU TELL ME THAT?!
YIKES!
NOW, NOW... WE STILL HAVE TIME. LET'S PUT OUR HEADS TOGETHER AND THINK.
DARN RIGHT!
I CAN'T LET THE BOSS FAIL!
HA HA
TICK
TICK
TICK
TICK
HMM...
YOU GUYS ARE A SAD LOT IN THIS STINKING HEAT.

WAFT
WHY NOT JUST HOLD AN ENDURANCE CONTEST?
GAD IT'S HOT!
PSHAA
BLUP BLUP
BLIP

WHAT'RE YOU DOING?!
ARE YOU THE DEVIL OR SOME-THING?
IT'S NOT ME.

WHO ELSE BUT YOU WOULD DO SOME-THING LIKE THIS...?
!

I'M NOT A DEVIL ...
SHAKY
HARU!

I HEARD YOU WERE WORKING HARD ON YOUR HOME-WORK...
DROOP
SO I THOUGHT THIS WOULD BE A GOOD CHANGE OF PACE.
TREMBLE

AN ENDURANCE CONTEST ISN'T WHAT I'D CALL...
...A CHANGE OF PACE, USUALLY!

WHISPER WHISPER
WHY DID YOU GO AHEAD AND GIVE IT TO HER?
THE MAFIA TAKES CARE OF ITS WOMEN.
TAKE GOOD CARE OF THE WOMAN WHO LOVES YOU.
HEY!
THIS ALL BEGAN BECAUSE SHE FELL IN LOVE WITH YOU, YOU KNOW.
THAT'S ALL RIGHT, REBORN... I'LL GO HOME ...
HUH?

TUP TUP TUP
I JUST WANT TO SAY...
I'M NOT ...
...A DEVIL ...
DOOOM
THE AIR SURE IS HEAVY ...

YOU SURE ARE POPULAR, TSUNA. HOW'D YOU MEET A GIRL LIKE THAT FROM SUCH A TOP SCHOOL?
TOP SCHOOL?
HUH?
THAT'S A MIDORI MIDDLE SCHOOL UNIFORM, ISN'T IT? AROUND HERE, IT'S ONE OF THE TOUGHEST ELITE SCHOOLS TO GET INTO.
OH...? THAT CRAZY GIRL?
SO HARU'S... SMART ...
THIS PROBLEM SEVEN MIGHT BE A CINCH FOR HER.
DA
WAIT UP...
I'LL GO ASK HARU!
SH

EEK!!
WHAT THE?!
SHE'S BEEN EAVES-DROPPING!

TING
PROBLEM SEVEN, RIGHT?
TING TING

WE STUDIED THIS. I THINK I CAN DO IT.
OHH—
CHOMP

FIVE MINUTES LATER
JUST A LITTLE MORE.

TEN MINUTES LATER
I'M ALMOST THERE.

ONE HOUR LATER
I'M JUST ABOUT DONE.

THREE HOURS LATER
I'M SORRY!
I DON'T KNOW HOW TO DO IT!
WHAT ?!
DARN YOU! IF YOU DON'T KNOW HOW, DON'T ACT LIKE YOU DO!
WE'RE IN TROUBLE- IT'S ALREADY DARK!
I THOUGHT I COULD SOLVE IT...
RATTLE
HUMM HUMM ♫
SWOP
WHO ARE YOU?
I'M LAMBO. ♪
CREEP CREEP
WHO AM I?
I'M LAMBO. ♪

HUH?
...?♪
...
!!

DON'T COME AROUND ...
DA DA DA
...WHEN WE'RE ALL UPSET!

I... I'M ...
JUST PASS-ING BY.
RUSH RUSH

WHAT'RE WE HAVING TODAY?
LIFT
YUCK... KIM-CHEE.
SHUKS
DON'T COME FOR DINNER!
SNAP

WOW! THIS KID IS CUTE...
KYAH HA
?
HEY!
YOU TWO! IF YOU'RE NOT GOING TO HELP WITH OUR HOME-WORK, LEAVE!

I'M...
SORRY...
KCHA KCHA

NOW, NOW... CALM DOWN, TSUNA, GOKUDERA.
IT'S ONLY JUST A SEVENTH-GRADE PROBLEM ...
IF WE ASK AN ADULT, THEY'D KNOW, RIGHT?

AN ADULT?
THE ONLY ADULT HERE IS...

DONN
ADULT LAMBO ?!
I HATE THIS.
NO, HE'S AN IDIOT ...
G-GRRR
THAT GUY'S STUPID ...

AH!
I KNOW AN ADULT WOMAN WHO CAN SOLVE THIS PROBLEM!

SERI-OUS?
OHH
YES. I HAD ODEN WITH HER RECENTLY.

SHE A REALLY PRETTY PERSON WHO LIKES TO COOK AS A HOBBY.
GREAT. SHE'S PERFECT.
A WOMAN AMONG WOMEN.
CLICK
HELLO... IS THIS BIANCHI?

WHAT?!
GASP
GAHHHH
EH?!
HO... HOLD IT!
YOU DON'T HAVE TO CALL BIANCHI!
SURPRISE
RING RING
SHE'S FAST!
SEEMS SHE WAS JUST PASSING BY.
GOKU-DERA!
DO DA DA DA DA DA
KCHA
EXCUSE ME...

SLAM
GA CHINK
SSHAN
UGH
WHEEZE
WHEEZE
I CAUGHT A GLIMPSE OF HER...

THAT SHYNESS COULD ONLY BE HAYATO.
I ONLY CAME TO SOLVE PROBLEM SEVEN.
HECK NO!
RRRGH
...
SUCH A HOPE-LESS CHILD.
BARTH
YOU'VE BECOME MUCH TOO CONSCIOUS OF YOUR OLDER SISTER'S FEMININITY.
POISON COOKING SOLVENT SAKURA RICECAKE.
KERCHA
BSHWAA
SSSS

AH
FW
ARGH!!
SHFFF

Rumble
No... cookies ...
WELL BIANCHI, CAN YOU SOLVE IT?
HMM ...
THIS DOESN'T MATTER AT ALL.
RIP

RRGH
WHAT THE ?!
YOU RIPPED IT!
TEAR
TEAR
WHAT'S IMPORTANT IS LOVE.
TEAR
IT DOES MATTER!
WE COULD FAIL BECAUSE OF THAT!
UWAAGH
CALM DOWN... I'LL MAKE A COPY OF MINE.
TEAR
TEAR
YOU COULDN'T SOLVE THE PROBLEM, AND NOW LOOK WHAT YOU'VE DONE!

KCHA
NO ONE ANSWERED THE DOOR, SO I LET MYSELF IN.
WHICH ONE IS IT, HARU?
THAT PROBLEM YOU COULDN'T SOLVE?
TA DAH

?
WH... WHO IS HE?
THIS IS MY DAD.
OH, MY FATHER TEACHES MATHEMATICS AT THE UNIVERSITY.
THAT'S WHY I CALLED HIM.
WHY DIDN'T YOU MENTION THAT FROM THE BEGINNING?
HE'D MAKE THE ULTIMATE HELPER!
HMM... THIS IS INDEED AT THE HIGHEST COLLEGE LEVEL.
BUT IT'S NOTHING I CAN'T SOLVE.
THE ANSWER IS THREE.
NO... FOUR.

YOU MISAPPLIED FOXTAIL'S FORMULA.
THE ANSWER IS FOUR.
WHAT? WHAT'RE YOU TALKING ABOUT, REBORN?!
THAT'S A UNIVERSITY PROFESSOR YOU'RE TALKING TO!
HUH?
THOSE SIDE-BURNS... I'VE SEEN THEM SOME-WHERE...
AH!
I REMEM-BER!
YOU'RE PROFESSOR BORIN, THE GENIUS MATHEMATICIAN!
TA-DAH
GRIN

HUH ?!
WHAT'RE YOU TALKING ABOUT?
FATHER?
I'M SURE OF IT! HE IS INDEED THE ONE WHO PERIODICALLY APPEARS IN ACADEMIA TO SOLVE EVERY SINGLE PROBLEM PREVIOUSLY CONSIDERED IMPOSSIBLE...
...THE MYSTERIOUS MATHE-MATICAL GENIUS KNOWN AS PROFESSOR BORIN!
mathematician Borin
(20??~)
maboroshi hakase tensai maboroshi hakase tensai maboroshi hakase tensai tensai maboroshi hakase tensai maboroshi hakase tensai maboroshi hakase tensai maboroshi tensai maboroshi hakase
THEY DO LOOK ALIKE, BUT YOU'VE GOT THE WRONG GUY...
N...NO, AND THE PROOF IS THAT I MADE A MISTAKE.
THE ANSWER IS FOUR.

HUH ...?
HUUH?

ARE YOU REALLY A MATHEMA-TICIAN?!
REBORN, YOU'RE AWE-SOME!

SPPUHH
HEY!

HA HA HA. HE WAS TALKING IN HIS SLEEP.
THINK ABOUT IT. HE'S JUST A BABY.
EH ...?
THERE ARE LOADS OF LOOK-ALIKES IN THIS WORLD.
YEAH, YOU'RE PROBABLY RIGHT!
THERE'S NO WAY, RIGHT?
I'M OVER-WHELMED!
A CHILD PRODIGY!
AND YET, TSUNA COULD NOT HELP BUT FEEL REBORN WAS A SUPERIOR TUTOR.

I AM BORIN.

Target 13
Shoichi Irie

SOMEN NOODLES AGAIN ?!
WE'VE BEEN HAVING NOTHING BUT LEFTOVERS FROM THE SUMMER GIFT-GIVING SEASON RECENTLY.
NOW, NOW...NO COMPLAINING.
THERE'S NOTHING WRONG- IT SAVES MONEY.
SLURP SLURP
SLURP SLURP

I LIKE YOUR NOODLES, MAMA.
I LIKE THEM, TOO.
MY, THANK YOU. I KNEW YOU AND BIANCHI WOULD, REBORN!
TSK.
AND SOMEONE ELSE LIKES MY SOMEN NOODLES, TOO.
RATTLE
HERE HE COMES NOW.
GA HA HA HA HA HA!
THAT RIDICULOUS ENTRANCE COULD ONLY BE...
IT'S ME, LAMBO!
BYOHHN
AT LEAST PUT ON YOUR HORNS ON STRAIGHT BEFORE COMING!
OOPS!
I DID THAT ON PURPOSE...
BUT I'LL FIX THEM FOR YOU...

I REALLY DID DO IT ON PURPOSE!
HUUU
DS
DIE, REBORN!
HE OPENED FIRED TO HIDE HIS EMBARRASS-MENT!
SNAP
!
KA
PSHUU
HYUU
PAP
UGH!
PLOCK
PSHUUU

EEEE!
PSHUUUU
...HE FLEW OFF.
...
SLURP SLURP
PSHUUU
EEEE!
BOOM
HUH...
DID YOU HEAR THAT?
WHY'RE YOU LOOKING SO TENSE, SHOICHI?

WHAT THE?
WHAT HAPPENED HERE?
IT'S A BABY!
IS... HE ALL RIGHT?
I DON'T BELIEVE IT. WHAT'S GOING ON?
DING DONG
WOULD YOU GET THAT, SHO-CHAN?
KCHA
WHO IS IT?

I WAS ASKED TO BRING THIS.
I'LL LEAVE IT HERE.
HUH?
UH...
DASH DASH DASH
FROM WHERE?
DASH
SLIDE

SOMEONE JUST MADE A SECRET DELIVERY ...
?!

CREAK

A Gift of Apology from the Bovinos
Pasta X 2
Olive oil X 3
Wine X 1
A GIFT OF APOLOGY?

WE REGRET THE TROUBLE OUR MAN LAMBO HAS CAUSED.
PLEASE ACCEPT THIS AS A SMALL TOKEN OF OUR APOLOGY. PLEASE GIVE THE PACKAGE WITH THE COW PRINT TO LAMBO.

LAMBO MUST BE THIS KID.
YEAH... BUT DIDN'T THIS COME TOO FAST...?

OH MY!
THERE'S A WAD OF BILLS!
...!

WINE, PASTA AND OLIVE OIL!
WOW

GT
ONK
SKRNCH
!
A COW PRINT ...
OH DEAR ...
THIS KID'S FAMILY MUST BE CRAZY.

!!
TH... THIS IS...

I APPRECIATE THE THOUGHT, BUT WHEN YOU TAKE THIS BOY BACK HOME, SHO-CHAN, RETURN THIS BOX, TOO.
M...
ME ?!
A MAN SHOULD GO, OF COURSE. WOMEN ARE FRAIL, YOU KNOW!
WHAT'S THIS?
SNATCH
OH, IT'S A KID'S TOY.

BUT I DON'T KNOW HIS ADDRESS, AND...
NO PROBLEM. I FOUND IT IN THAT BOY'S POCKET.

IT SAYS REBORN... I WONDER IF IT'S A FOREIGNER'S PLACE...?
Orders Target:
Reborn Sawada
Address:
12 OO-cho
IT'S QUITE NEARBY.

IF ANYTHING HAPPENS, WE'LL RUSH RIGHT OVER.
I'LL LEND YOU MY CELL PHONE, SO CALL US.
WHEN ANYTHING HAPPENS, IT'S ALWAYS ME...

THIS MUST BE THE PLACE ...
SAWADA

!!

BLINK

ARE YOU HERE TO KILL HIM?

?!

!
WHAT'S THE MATTER, BIANCHI?
REBORN.

SIGH

CIAO-SU!

SHOICHI'S IMAGES OF REBORN
...!!!
OR

!!!
GULP GULP
WHAT IS IT?

UH... ER... I...
GULP.

HUH!
GRAB
REBORN!
!!

GA HA HA HA HA. LAMBO'S HORNS...
GRAB
...CAN BECOME POWERFUL WEAPONS!
BITE THE DUST...
SWISH
REBORN!
GLORP
KREENG
THOK
Leon
...
!
TOPPLE
AGH...
BRAANG
...!
SORRY TO BOTHER YOU!
DASH DASH DASH
BRAANG

SHWIFF
BEEP
REBORN WAS A BABY!
HUH?
A BABY?
BUT HE WAS DRINKING BEER!
AND HE'S A CRAZY STRONG FIGHTER!
AH...
YOU MEAN A "BABE," NOT A BABY, RIGHT? A REALLY STRONG BABE?
NO!
SO SHE'S NOT REALLY THAT STRONG? DID LITTLE LAMBO WAKE UP? IS HE OKAY?
HE'S ALMOST DEAD!
HUH?
THE CHILD ON YOUR BACK?
!
LAMBO IS A CHILD ...
...WHO PERSEVERES!
BLINK

I'LL MAKE YOU GO BOOM THE NEXT TIME FOR SURE!
BOOM! BOOM! BOOOOM!
HUH!
DARN YOU!
VOOP
VOOP
VOOP
BLORP
PFF
PFF
PFF
B-B-BOOM
GPYAAGH!!
...!!

REBORN TOOK OUT LAMBO!

IT'S NICE TO BE A CELEBRITY...
?!
AND WHAT DID HE BUY FOR HIM?
HE DIDN'T BUY ANY-THING!

THOSE CELEBS... ARE THEY SHOOTING FIREWORKS IN THE AFTER-NOON?
NO!

FROM THE MORN-ING?
THOSE AREN'T FIRE-WORKS!
SHO-CHAN, YOU'RE VERY ENERGETIC TODAY.

HEY!

WHO JUST BLEW SOME-THING UP?!
IF STRANGE RUMORS START GOING AROUND, I'LL GET KICKED OUT OF SCHOOL!

HEY!
STUPID COW.
BIANCHI, WHY'RE YOU DRESSED LIKE THAT?!
THE NEIGH-BORS WILL THINK YOU'RE CRAZY.
A NORMAL PERSON!
!
THAT PERSON MIGHT ...
SHFFL
!
UWAAAGH
...?!
BOOM
AH!
HUH ?!
PSHHH
PSHHH
PSHHH
PSHHH

SSSSS
SSSSS
HERE WE GO AGAIN ...
SSSSS
JUST WHEN I WAS ENJOYING THE FOOD AT THE INN...
SSSSS
!!!
THUD
THIS WAY?
... BECAME... AN ADULT...
I'M PROUD OF YOU, SHO-CHAN. BUT YOU SHOULDN'T BOAST TOO MUCH ABOUT YOURSELF.
NOT ME!

GOOD DAY, YOUNG TENTH GENERATION OF THE VONGOLA FAMILY.
SO THAT EXPLOSION WAS LAMBO, JUST AS I THOUGHT.
!
!
HERE WE GO AGAIN ...
I'LL BE ON MY WAY NOW...
IT'S... OKAY. I EXPLAINED TO BIANCHI ABOUT YOU.
SORRY ABOUT BEFORE, LAMBO.

YOU SEE, THIS IS WHAT THAT KID WILL LOOK LIKE IN TEN YEARS.
SEE? DO YOU UNDER-STAND NOW, BIANCHI?
BIANCHI ...?
SO YOU WERE STILL ALIVE.
BSHWAA
ROMEO ...
IT'S NOT HIM, I SAID!
IT'S AS THOUGH A SWITCH IN HER TURNS ON.
DASH
RUN, LAMBO!
DASH
WHOOSH
I'LL KILL YOU!
DASH
DASH
DASH
MOM... I HAVE A BAD FEELING ABOUT THIS...

SWOOSH
LUNGE
!
PING
!!!
GRAZE
WHAT THE?!
HUH ?!
PING
PING
BIANCHI'S MARKS-MANSHIP WAS THE WORST.
YOU NEVER KNOW WHERE HER BULLETS WILL FLY.
HEY ...!
PING

RAT-TAT-TAT-
TAT-TAT
VOOP

MOM... I'M GONNA DIE...
A BULLET GRAZED ME... MOM! A BULLET...
HYA HA HA HA HA HA HA
PING
PING
PING
?!
HELLO? THIS IS YOUR LOVELY SISTER. MOM COULDN'T FOLLOW WHAT YOU WERE TALKING ABOUT, SO SHE LEFT TO GO SHOPPING.
!

MY...YOU'VE LEARNED TO TELL JOKES, SHOICHI... I WAS WORRIED ABOUT YOU FOR A WHILE...
I'VE GOT A DATE WITH MY FRIENDS, TOO, SO SEE YOU.
CLICK
BEEP BEEP
GASP
RAT-TAT-TAT-TAT
PING
PING
PING
DO SOMETHING, REBORN!
AT THIS RATE, SOMEONE IS GOING TO GET KILLED!
HAWA
27

YOU CAN TAKE CARE OF IT, RIGHT, TSUNA?
CLICK
!
W... WAIT!
HOLD IT.
BANG
HUFF
HUFF
THUD
...
!
UWAAAAGH!!
CRASH

SHUFFL
GASP.
WHA ?!
TREMBLE TREMBLE
HUH?
SPROING
Y-YI-
Y-YIKES!
TREMBLE TREMBLE
FOAM FOAM
RE-BORN!
I WILL STOP THE FIGHT WITH DEATHPER-ATION!
RIP
...!
THE SECRET TO STOPPING A FIGHT IS TO MAKE SOMEONE LOSE THE WILL TO FIGHT.
SHOOTING BOTH CHEEKS ...
BANG BANG
BSS BSS
...!

*Niramekko is a staring game where each player tries to make the other laugh first. The first to laugh is the loser.

I'M TICKED OFF!
SPLAT
HUH ...!

CRASH
IT DOESN'T WORK ON BIANCHI, I GUESS.

THAT NIGHT ...

WHAT'S WRONG? WHY IS SHOICHI MOANING IN HIS SLEEP?
WELL ...
A LOT HAPPENED.
UNGH... UNGH...

WHOK
WHOK
WHOK
PSHOO
BOOM
BOOM
BOOM

IN THE END, THE GIFT OF APOLOGY WAS NEVER RETURNED AND LEFT UNDER SHOICHI'S DESK.
SHOICHI FELT HIS NIGHTMARES WOULD NOT CEASE UNTIL HE RETURNED THE GIFT.

Where'd Romeo go...?

Target 14
Ryohei Sasagawa

SIGH... WHY'D I OVERSLEEP FOR THE FIRST DAY OF SCHOOL?
SIGH
I'LL STILL BE TARDY NO MATTER HOW MUCH I RUSH.
YOU WON'T KNOW UNTIL YOU TRY, RIGHT?
CLICK
HUH? YOU!
WAIT A MINUTE!
...!!!
BANG
RROOOOAR!!
DASH
DASH
I'LL MAKE IT TO SCHOOL WITH DEATHPER-ATION!

BA
WHAT'S THAT?
TH... THAT'S ...
LOSER TSUNA IN 7TH GRADE CLASS A.
!
RROOAR!!
DASH DASH DASH
HOLD IT.
GR AB
UGH
HUH ?!
DASH DASH
DASH DASH
PSSSFF

SN
YOU HAVE GREATER POWER, STAMINA AND PASSION THAN I HAD HEARD!
A TRUE ONCE-IN-A-CENTURY PROSPECT!
AP
DARN THAT REBORN ...
PSSFF
I MADE IT IN TIME, BUT I'M GOING TO BE SHAMED AGAIN...
OGLE
YOU'RE DEFINITE-LY THE REAL DEAL...
?!
YIKES! I HOOKED SOMEONE ALONG THE WAY...
ARE YOU... ALL RIGHT?
TUMBLE
?!
HUH?
JOIN OUR CLUB!
TSUNA SAWADA!
EH?
WHY ...
WHY DO YOU KNOW MY NAME?

BECAUSE I'VE HEARD ABOUT YOUR HUSTLE FROM MY YOUNGER SISTER.
Y... YOUNGER SISTER?

BROTHER.
WHAT'S THE MATTER, KYOKO?!
?!

KYOKO...? THAT'S AN AWFULLY FAMILIAR-SOUNDING NAME...
KYOKO... KYOKO...

OH... YOU DROPPED YOUR BAG ON THE STREET!
THAT KYOKO ?!

OH, GOOD MORNING, TSUNA.
THANKS.
HUH?
UH...

?
WHY'RE THE TWO OF YOU TOGETHER?

OH... BROTHER, YOU'RE NOT CAUSING TSUNA TROUBLE, ARE YOU?
NO, I'M NOT!
!
NO... NOT HER... BROTHER ...?

WHAT ?!
THIS GUY IS KYOKO'S BIG BROTHER ...?!

TSUNA, YOU CAN JUST IGNORE BROTHER'S BOXING STORIES, OKAY?
SPEAKING OF WHICH, I HAVEN'T INTRODUCED MYSELF YET.
BOX-ING ...?

I AM RYOHEI SASAGAWA, CAPTAIN OF THE BOXING CLUB!
MY MOTTO IS: "TO THE LIMIT"!

SUCH... PASSION!

WELCOME TO THE CLUB, TSUNA SAWADA!
HUH?
GRAB
I UH...

NO, BROTHER... YOU MUSTN'T FORCE TSUNA TO JOIN...
I'M NOT FORCING HIM!
RIGHT... TSUNA?
GRRR
UH-HUH.

WHAT SHOULD I DO?
I CAN'T BOX AT ALL, BUT I DON'T WANT KYOKO'S OLDER BROTHER TO HATE ME...

I'LL BE WAITING AT THE GYM AFTER SCHOOL, THEN!
UM ...
WAIT ...
ON SECOND THOUGHT, I...

HE CAN BE CRUDE, I KNOW. BUT HE HAS A GENTLE SIDE YOU WOULDN'T EXPECT.
!

BUT YOU'RE TERRIFIC, TSUNA.
I'M HAPPY, TOO...
HUH?

IT'S BEEN A LONG TIME SINCE I'VE SEEN BROTHER LOOK SO HAPPY.
IT JUST BECAME A LOT HARDER TO SAY NO!
DOOM

IT'S NO GOOD... I CAN'T BOX...

BUT I DON'T WANT KYOKO'S OLDER BROTHER TO HATE ME...
HOW SHOULD I TURN HIM DOWN ...?

SAWADA! I'VE BEEN WAITING FOR YOU!
RATTLE
AH!
GASP

A VETERAN MUAY THAI FIGHTER CAME ALL THE WAY FROM THAILAND...
...AFTER HEARING ABOUT YOUR REPUTA-TION.
HUH? A VETERAN FROM THAI-LAND?

MEET COACH PAO PAO.
TRUMPET!!
YOU ...!

I WANT TO SEE A HEAD-TO-HEAD FIGHT BETWEEN THE NEW GUY AND THE CLUB'S CAPTAIN.
HEY.
WHAT'RE YOU TALKING ABOUT?
YOU PLAN ON...
...MAKING ME BOX ?!
NATURALLY.
YOU NEED GET A BIT STRONGER ...
YEAH, SPARRING WITH ME MIGHT BE A GOOD WAY TO TEST YOUR ABILITY, SAWADA.
HUH?
NOT YOU, TOO, RYOHEI!
HOLD ON A MINUTE ...
GOOD LUCK, TSUNA!
DON'T LOSE.
TENTH GENERA-TION!
HEY!
GASP
YOU ALL CAME ...
IT'S GETTING HARDER AND HARDER TO SAY NO...
HUH?
TRUMPET!!
DOESN'T ANYBODY REALIZE THAT'S REBORN ...?
NNNGH

HERE I COME, TSUNA SAWADA!
I WON'T HOLD BACK!
GASP
Fight! Tsuna!
Tenth Generation!
WHAT AM I DOING?
CLANG
W
PA
THUD

KEEP YOUR GUARD UP, SAWADA!
THAT'S NOT THE PROBLEM, THIS IS THE BEST I CAN DO...
I WANT TO GO HOME ALREADY...
!
CLICK
REBORN!
WAIT A MINUTE... IF HE SHOOTS ME AND I BECOME DEATHPERATE...
THUMP
I'M GOING TO WIN WITH DEATHPERATION!
RROOAR
IT'LL GO LIKE THIS...
WHUMP
WHUP
THUMP
UGH
UGH
UGH
THEN THIS...
BROTHER!
I'M... DUST...
THUNK

THAT WAS MEAN, TSUNA! LOOK WHAT YOU DID TO MY BROTHER!
I HATE YOU!
NNGH
NOT GOOD!

NO!
NO! NO! DON'T SHOOT ME!
SSASA
BANG
THEN I'LL DO IT THIS WAY.
?
HUH?
CRASH

HUH ?!
YOU HIT RYOHEI WITH THE DEATHPER-ATION SHOT?!
IF I SHOOT BOTH OF YOU, YOU'RE EVEN, RIGHT?
IF HE SHOT RYOHEI WITH THE DEATHPER-ATION SHOT,
WITH ALL OF HIS PASSION, HE'LL ...
SLUMP
SLUMP
...!

DOOM
UWAAGH!!
I'M GOING TO BE KILLED!
IN AN INSTANT!
WHAT'S THE MATTER, SAWADA?
CAN'T YOU GET UP?
HUH?

IF YOU CAN GET UP, LET'S CONTINUE!
WHAT?
HE HASN'T CHANGED AT ALL...
HE WAS HIT WITH THE DEATHPER-ATION SHOT, BUT HE HASN'T CHANGED A BIT...
WHICH MEANS ...
AH!
COULD IT MEAN ?!

THE DEATHPERATION SHOT HAS NO EFFECT ON PEOPLE WHO ARE DEATHPERATE TO BEGIN WITH?!
DOOOM

RYOHEI SASAGAWA...
AN IMPRESSIVE FELLOW.
WHY DID SASAGAWA SEMPAI GO DOWN JUST NOW?
HE SLIPPED, RIGHT?
HE LIVES WITH DEATHPERATION...
HE REALLY DOES LIVE "TO THE LIMIT"...
YOU'RE NEXT, TSUNA.
BANG
GO
TSUNA'S REGRET AT THAT MOMENT...
WAS NOT HOW HE PERFORMED IN THE SPARRING MATCH...
BUT THAT HE COULD NOT TURN DOWN THE INVITATION TO JOIN THE CLUB...
SLUMP

R
WITH DEATHPER-ATION,
I WILL TURN DOWN THE INVITATION TO JOIN THE CLUB!
!
?
OH...
I WON'T ASK YOU WHY...
I
P
BECAUSE I BELIEVE TWO MEN CAN TELL EVERY-THING WITH THEIR FISTS.
JOIN THE CLUB, SAWADA!
S
NO WAY !!!
SKRRM
NAP
GRRR

SHWA
YOU SLIPPED MY "TO THE LIMIT" STRAIGHT RIGHT!
I LIKE YOU EVEN MORE NOW!
ALL THE MORE REASON TO MAKE YOU JOIN, SAWADA!
WOP
WOP
WOP
NO...!
WAY!
INCREDIBLE! HE'S SLIPPING SASAGAWA SEMPAI'S "TO THE LIMIT" ATTACK...!
WHO IS THAT GUY?!
THE WAY TSUNA IS DODGING THOSE ATTACKS IS INCREDIBLE, BUT...
THAT'S NO ORDINARY FIGHTER'S ATTACK...
IT'S THAT OF AN ASSASSIN...
GRRR
JOIN! JOIN! JOIN! JOIN!
NO! NO! NO! NO!
I REFUSE!
POW
GWAAGH!!

SL
AM
WAY TO GO, TENTH GENERA-TION.
!
YIKES! I WENT AND DID IT!
PSSSFF
GASP

I MAY NEVER... BE ABLE TO TALK TO KYOKO AGAIN.
SIGH
SIGH
I LIKE YOU ALL THE MORE, SAWADA!
?!

YOU HAVE PLATINUM BOXING INSTINCTS! I'M GOING TO RECRUIT YOU YET!
OH, YOU LOOK SO HAPPY, BROTHER!
HUFF
HUFF
WHAT?! HE ENDED UP LIKING ME INSTEAD!
GASP
I LIKE WHAT I SAW, RYOHEI SASAGAWA.
?!
WANT TO JOIN THE FAMILY?
?
H..HEY! NOW YOU'RE SCOUT-ING HIM?!
REBORN WAS GETTING GREEDY.

TRUMPET

Target 15
Dr. Shamal

DING DONG
TRUMPET
TRUMPET
WOOZY
HUH?
I FEEL FAINT ...
MAYBE IT'S THE FLU...
OH WELL, IF IT IS, THAT'S OKAY 'CUZ I CAN SKIP SCHOOL...
!!
WHAT!
DOOOM
WHAT'S THIS ?!

THAT'S AN INCURABLE DISEASE CALLED THE SKULLITIS.
BOIIING
YOU'RE GOING TO DIE, TSUNA.
JUST LIKE THAT ?!
WHY'RE YOU BRINGING ME SUCH BAD NEWS?
ARE YOU THE GRIM REAPER OR SOMETHING?
THAT WAS YOUR WORST ENTRANCE YET!

DO YOU REMEMBER HOW MANY DEATHPERATION SHOTS YOU'VE TAKEN TO THE HEAD SO FAR?
HUH? HOW... MANY ...?
I WOULDN'T KNOW!

EXACTLY TEN!
IT'S SAID THAT IF YOU'VE BEEN KILLED TEN TIMES BY THE DEATHPERATION SHOT, TERRIBLE THINGS WILL HAPPEN.

I NEVER THOUGHT IT'D BE AN INCURABLE DISEASE...
TOO BAD.
DON'T TALK LIKE I'M ALREADY DEAD!
I MEAN, WHY DID YOU KEEP SOME-THING SO IMPORTANT FROM ME?
IF I HAD KNOWN ...
SIGH.
I'M GOING HOME.
YOU'RE TAKING IT BETTER THAN I THOUGHT YOU WOULD.
WHY SHOULDN'T I? I DON'T BELIEVE IT'S AN INCURABLE DISEASE.
IT'LL JUST WASH OFF.

WHAT THE ?!
YOU'VE NEVER SCORED 100%!
THE SKULL'S TALKING!

READ THIS WAY
SKULLITIS IS A RARE DISEASE WHERE UNTELLABLE SECRETS AND EMBARRASSING EPISODES APPEAR AS WORDS ALL OVER YOUR BODY UNTIL THE DAY YOU DIE.
IT'S ALSO KNOWN AS THE "SHAME YOU TO DEATH" DISEASE.
HUH?
THAT'S ...
THAT'S RIDICUL-OUS!
SCRUB SCRUB SCRUB
!
ANOTHER ONE!
AND THIS IS...!
DRIP
YOU SKIP SCHOOL ON DAYS WHEN YOU'RE SUPPOSED TO GET A SHOT
DRIP DRIP
AN EMBAR-RASSING SECRET ONLY YOU'RE SUPPOSED TO KNOW, RIGHT?
GASP
!
THEN THIS REALLY IS A DISEASE ?!
DIDN'T I JUST SAY SO? JUST SO YOU KNOW, YOU'LL DIE IN AN HOUR AFTER THE SYMPTOMS OF SKULLITIS APPEAR.
YOU HAVE ANOTHER THIRTY MINUTES OR SO BEFORE YOU DIE, I THINK.
GAAN
WHAT?!

HOW CAN THAT BE!
I DON'T WANT TO DIE YET...!
ESPECIALLY NOT WITH MESSAGES OF HOW MUCH OF A LOSER I AM ENGRAVED ALL OVER MY BODY!
GIGGLE GIGGLE
GIGGLE GIGGLE
GIGGLE GIGGLE
HELP ME, REBORN!
I CAN'T HELP YOU.
AAAH... TELL ME YOU'RE LYING TO ME!
WAGH
THIS SUCKS! MY WHOLE LIFE SUCKS!
THERE DOES EXIST ONE WAY TO SAVE YOURSELF.
?!
WHAT DID YOU JUST SAY?!
I HAVE AN ACQUAINTANCE, A DOCTOR WHO'S VERY GOOD WITH INCURABLE DISEASES. IF I SUMMON HIM, HE MIGHT BE ABLE TO DO SOMETHING.
WHY DIDN'T YOU SAY THAT SOONER?
HURRY AND CALL HIM!
HUH?

HEY.
THAT'S NO WAY TO ASK. WHAT?
HEY.
SPLAT
I WAS JUST KIDDING, REBORN SIR. YOU ARE A CLASSY ASSASSIN.
PLEASE SUMMON THAT DOCTOR.
IF YOU'RE CURED, WILL YOU MAKE IT INTO THE TOP TEN IN YOUR CLASS ON THE NEXT TEST?
HUH?!
WHAT AN OPPORTUNIST...
IF YOU DON'T WANT TO...
I WILL, I WILL, I WILL!
I'LL MAKE IT!
STOP IT!
DIE.
UGH!
CRASH
BANG
WHAT THE...
...HECK'S GOING ON?!
WHUMP WHUMP WHUMP
!!
WHO...
WHO'S THERE...?

DID HE FALL VICTIM TO POISON COOKING ?!
THUMP
QUIVER
QUIVER
IT'S BEEN A LONG TIME SINCE I DID A HIT THAT BENEFITED SOCIETY.
THUMP THUMP
WHA?
BIANCHI!!
DON'T GO KILLING PEOPLE ...
...IN MY HOUSE!
THAT'S HOW GIRLS SHOULD BE.
DROOP
PEEL
YOU ALWAYS WERE A TOMBOY.
!
HE'S ALIVE!

I LOVE YOU EVEN MORE NOW.
SMOOCH
SRING
WHAT THE ?!
!
DIE!
WHAM
CRASH
ROLL ROLL
UGH.
WHO THE...
...HECK IS THIS INTRUDER ...?
THE DOCTOR I TOLD YOU ABOUT EARLIER.
HUH ?!
I SUMMONED HIM FROM ITALY FOR YOU.
MEET DR. SHAMAL.

WAH
YOU'RE SUCH A SHY ONE.
C'mon, kiss me, baby.
!
BACK OFF!
SPLAT
AS YOU CAN SEE, HE'S A WOMANIZER AND AN INCORRIGIBLE KISSER.
CAN THIS GUY ...
GASP
REALLY CURE AN INCURABLE DISEASE ...?
I MEAN, IS HE EVEN A REAL DOCTOR?
WHISPER WHISPER
YUP. HE'S HELPED ME BEFORE, TOO.
HUH?
YOU CONTRACTED AN INCURABLE DISEASE, TOO?

IT WAS SHAMAL WHO DELIVERED ME AT BIRTH.
WHEN YOU WERE BORN ?!
AN OBSTETRICIAN... I SUPPOSE I SHOULD'VE GUESSED.
SHAMAL, THIS IS TSUNA, THE ONE WITH SKULLITIS.

HNH?
OH YEAH... RIGHT... THAT'S WHAT YOU CALLED ME HERE FOR, WASN'T IT?
SORRY ABOUT THAT... I TEND TO HAVE A ONE-TRACK MIND AND FORGET ABOUT EVERYTHING ELSE...
HMM
NICE TO MEET YOU.
PARDON ME.
HMM... HMM...
HUH ?!
PLAT
HUH ?!

SORRY, I DON'T TREAT MEN.
GASP
WHAT?!
OH, THAT'S RIGHT.
NNNGH
SAY WHAT ?!
WAIT! YOU CAN'T BE SERIOUS!
ARE YOU GONNA LET ME DIE JUST BECAUSE OF THAT?!
WHAT DO YOU MEAN "JUST"? IT'S A HUGE DIFFERENCE.

!
ARGH.
IT'S SPREAD TO BOTH MY ARMS!
AARGH! HOW EMBARRASSING! THAT TOO...?
CAN'T TASTE THE DIFFERENCE BETWEEN HAM AND SAUSAGES.
AFRAID OF MOTHS.
LOST 245 STRAIGHT INDIVIDUAL COMPETITIONS.
CAN'T SLEEP IN TOTAL DARKNESS.
SLIPPED ON A BANANA
CAN'T MULTIPLY BY SEVEN.
CAN'T DRINK COFFEE.
PLEASE, DR. SHAMAL! HELP ME! I DON'T WANT TO DIE! NOT IN THIS SHAMEFUL WAY!
HEY YOU!
I DON'T WANT A GUY HUGGING ME! IT MAKES MY SKIN CRAWL!
GRAB
I'VE EXAMINED A MILLION PATIENTS, BUT NOT ONE OF THEM WAS MALE.
ZERO EXCEPTIONS-THEN, OR EVER.
GIVE IT UP.
THIS CAN'T BE HAPPEN-ING!
POOR BOY...
BIANCHI!
PHUUU
YOU'RE ENJOYING THIS, AREN'T YOU?!

KISS ME, BIANCHI!
BUG OFF!
!
WAAGH!!
IT'S... HOPELESS...
EXCUSE ME...
!
IS THIS A BAD TIME?
INTRODUCTORY SERIES
BLOOD AND TEARS BOXING
VOLUME 1
WH... WHAT BRINGS YOU HERE?

KYOKO!
BROTHER HASN'T GIVEN UP AT ALL ON TRYING TO RECRUIT YOU FOR THE BOXING CLUB.
HE ASKED ME TO GIVE YOU THIS BOOK ON BOXING.
!
CHOKE
I'M... TOUCHED...
REGARDLESS OF WHY, KYOKO CAME TO SEE ME BEFORE I DIE!
TSUNA... ARE YOU INTO BODY PAINTING?!
!!
SHWFF
NO, THIS ...!
SHWFF
..ISN'T BODY PAINTING!
DON'T LOOK.

OH...
YOU'RE CUTE ...
I'LL GIVE YOU A KISS.
PUCKER
SHFF
HEY!
HOLD ON. WHAT KIND OF ANIMAL ARE YOU?!
STAY AWAY FROM KYOKO!
WHY? WHAT'S IT MATTER TO YOU?
YOU'RE GOING TO DIE IN FIVE MINUTES.
GULP

AH HA HA. YOU SAY THE SILLIEST THINGS.
STRANGE MAN.
HUH?
YOU SEE, SHE LIKES ME. YOUR KISS IS WAITING RIGHT HERE.
GASP
THIS CAN'T BE!
IF I DIE NOW, KYOKO WILL FALL PREY TO SHAMAL...
SMOOCH
I DON'T WANT THAT TO HAPPEN! ANY... THING BUT THAT! THAT MUST NEVER...
AT THAT MOMENT, TSUNA'S MENTAL STATE BECAME INFINITELY CLOSE TO THAT STATE.

IF THAT'S HOW IT'S GOING TO BE...
I'D DEATHPERATELY...

WISH I HAD DEATHPERATELY GOTTEN RID OF THE VERMIN COMING AROUND KYOKO.
IF I KNEW THIS WAS GOING TO HAPPEN, I DEATHPERATELY WANT TO...
THAT TSUNA ...
HE'S TRYING TO BECOME DEATHPERATE WITHOUT THE DEATHPERATION SHOT.
RIP
ROAR!!
I'LL PROTECT KYOKO WITH DEATHPERATION!
...ARE
DOGS...
WENT TO THE HOSPITAL WITH A BEAN STUCK IN HIS NOSE.
TRIPS AND FALLS AT LEAST ONCE A WEEK.
OFTEN DISRESPECTED BY YOUNGER KIDS
TAUNTED AND CALLED A SAIYAJIN
OCTOPUS AND
85 STRAIGHT LOSSES IN TEAM SPORTS
ONCE READ IMPORTANT AS IMPOTENT
CAN'T TASTE THE DIFFERENCE BETWEEN BUTTER AND MARGARINE.

!!
NOW YOU'RE SAYING STRANGE THINGS, TOO, TSUNA.
WOW... YOU HAVE ALL SORTS OF THINGS WRITTEN ON YOU...
WAH
THIS IS EMBARRASSING!
BARING MY SECRETS, AND BECOMING DEATHPERATE!
TSUNA, YOU REALLY ARE A LOSER WITH NO GUTS.
THAT'S RIGHT! I'M JUST A LOSER. A LOSER!
I'M GOING TO DIE A LOSER!
WAAAAGH
LEAVE ME ALONE ALREADY!

OKAY, OKAY, I'LL CURE YOU.
SCARED OF SLUGS.
WHAT'S A LEAP YEAR?
OCTOPUS AND...

WE DON'T HAVE TIME.
HURRY AND PUT YOUR SHIRT BACK ON.
!

DR. SHAMAL ...
STAY THERE AND BE STILL.
UH... CAN YOU REALLY CURE AN INCURABLE DISEASE?

I WAS BORN WITH A PREDISPOSITION FOR ATTRACTING BACTERIA AND VIRUSES.
RIGHT NOW, I'M INFECTED WITH 666 INCURABLE DISEASES.
HUH ?!

IF YOU'RE WONDERING WHY I'M IMMUNE, IT'S BECAUSE TWO EXACTLY OPPOSITE DISEASES WILL CANCEL EACH OTHER OUT.
MINUS
PLUS
FOR EXAMPLE, BY BEING AFFLICTED AT THE SAME TIME WITH A DISEASE THAT CAUSES A HIGH FEVER AND A DISEASE THAT LOWERS THE BODY TEMPERATURE, MY BODY TEMPERATURE REMAINS NORMAL.
IS IT POSSIBLE TO HAVE 333 PAIRS OF EXACTLY OPPOSITE DISEASES?!
FLIP
JUST SO YOU KNOW, THE EXACT OPPOSITE OF SKULLITIS IS ANGELITIS.

THIS IS THE ONE.
A CAPSULE?
FLICK
POP
BZZZ
THE TRIDENT...
...MOSQUITO!

BZZZ
A MOSQUITO?!
SHAMAL IS ORDINARILY A DOCTOR, BUT HE'S ALSO AN ASSASSIN KNOWN AS "TRIDENT SHAMAL."
SHAMAL'S SPECIAL KILLING TECHNIQUE IS MANIPULATING THE TRIDENT MOSQUITO THAT CARRIES 666 DIFFERENT INCURABLE DISEASES TO KILL PEOPLE WITH ILLNESS.
SCARY!!

DO YOUR THING, ANGEL MOSQUITO!
OKAY.
PTAT
AAGH... IT'S SUCKING!
THAT SHOULD CANCEL OUT THE DISEASE.
!!
THE WORDS ARE DISAPPEARING...
FADE
THANK YOU, DR. SHAMAL!
ENJOY YOUR LIFE TO THE FULLEST.
BUT... WHAT MADE YOU SUDDENLY DECIDE TO TREAT ME?
BECAUSE WHEN I READ THE SECRETS ON YOUR BACK, I FELT SORRY FOR YOU...
HUH?
SEEMS YOU'VE NEVER SPOKEN TO A GIRL UNTIL YOU SPOKE TO KYOKO, EH?
IT'S JUST TOO WRETCHED.
KYOKO WAS THE FIRST GIRL HE EVER SPOKE TO (2 MONTHS AGO).
LEAVE ME ALONE!
TSUNA ESCAPED FROM A CLOSE CALL THANKS TO BEING A LOSER.

Okay, time to hit the nightlife...

Target 16 Kyoya Hibari

Kyoya Hibari
ALL RIGHT, THEN...
CARRY ON.

ISN'T IT ODD, THOUGH, FOR A COMMITTEE TO USE THE RECEPTION ROOM?
YOU THINK SO, TOO?
I SMELL A CONSPIRACY.
ARE YOU GUYS THE "GOOD FRIENDS COMMITTEE"?
IT'S SUPPOSED TO BE JUST ONE REPRESENTATIVE FROM EACH COMMITTEE ...

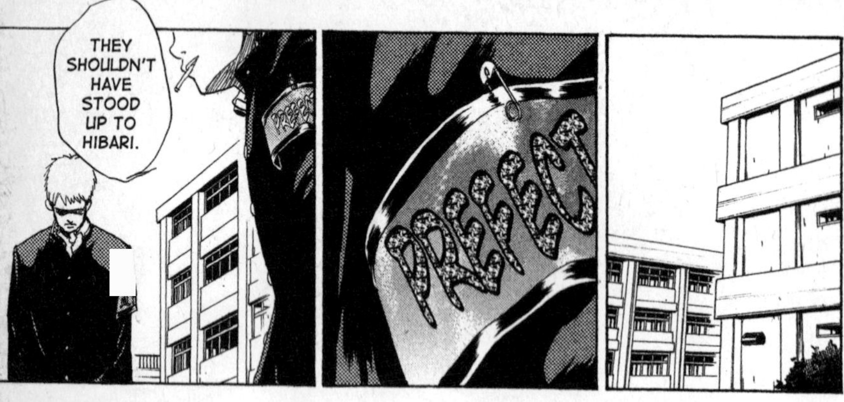
THEY SHOULDN'T HAVE STOOD UP TO HIBARI.

THIS IS WHAT HAPPENS WHEN THEY TRY TO GANG UP ON HIBARI.
UGH ...

YAWN.
Dental
KYOYA HIBARI.
INTRIGUING.

IS IT ALREADY AUTUMN ...?
SUMMER BREAK WENT BY IN A FLASH. I MISS IT ALREADY...
WE SPENT THE WHOLE BREAK IN REMEDIAL.
ISN'T THAT STUPID COW-BOY'S CONSTANT NAGGING FOR GRAPES GETTING TO YOU RECENTLY?
GRAPES.

CHEST-NUTS ARE GOOD, TOO!
OUCH!!
SWOOSH
PRICK
SWOOSH
PRICK
OW... OUCH!
IS THAT YOU, REBORN?!
TURN
OW!
CIAO-SU.
GASP
OUCH! OUCH! YOU'RE POKING ME!
PRICKLE
PRICKLE
PRICKLE
PRICKLE
THIS IS MY AUTUMN CAMOUFLAGE SUIT FOR SECRET OPERATIONS.
ONE HUNDRED PEOPLE OUT OF A HUNDRED WOULD NOTICE YOU!
I TOLD YOU NOT TO SHOW UP AT THE SCHOOL!
SQUEAK
I'M GOING TO CREATE A HIDEOUT FOR OUR FAMILY.
HUH?!

OH... SOUNDS INTERESTING. A SECRET BASE, EH?
YOU'RE SUCH A KID!

A HIDE-OUT SOUNDS GREAT.
THE FAMILY DEFINITELY NEEDS A HIDEOUT.
THEN IT'S SET.
WAIT...
...A MINUTE.

YOU CAN'T BE SERIOUS!
A HIDE-OUT, LIKE THE MAFIA?!

WHERE ARE WE GOING TO SET IT UP? IN THE HILLS OUT BACK?!
OF COURSE NOT!
IN THE SCHOOL'S RECEPTION ROOM.
?!

THE RECEPTION ROOM IS HARDLY EVER USED.
IT'S FURNISHED, AND IT HAS A GREAT VIEW. IT'S THE PERFECT SETUP.

WE'LL HAVE TO START BY REARRANG-ING THE TABLES.
I'M SITTING TO THE BOSS'S IMMEDIATE RIGHT.
ARE THEY SERIOUS ...?!

READ THIS WAY

Reception Room

CLICK
OHH...
I NEVER KNEW SUCH A NICE ROOM EXISTED ...

WHO'RE YOU?

!

HE'S
...

DESPITE BEING A PREFECT, HE STANDS ATOP THE JUVENILE GANG WORLD...
KYOYA HIBARI, A.K.A. HIBARI ...!

WHO THE HECK IS HE?
GOKU-DERA, WAIT ...

WOULD YOU MIND PUTTING OUT THAT CIGARETTE IN THE PRESENCE OF THE HEAD PREFECT?
EITHER WAY, YOU'RE NOT LEAVING HERE UNSCATHED.

WAH !!
WHAT WAS THAT, YOU?!

WHOOSH
SNIP
PUT IT OUT.

WAH
WHO IS THIS GUY?!
HE'LL BEAT THE HECK OUT OF YOU WITH HIS COLLAPS-IBLE TONFA.
I'VE HEARD OF HIM...
IF HIBARI DOESN'T LIKE YOU, IT DOESN'T MATTER WHO YOU ARE...

I HATE WEAK BOTTOM FEEDERS LIKE YOU WHO BAND TOGETHER.
WHEN I SEE THEM...

I WANNA TAKE THEM DOWN.

ZOKK
JERK!

THIS GUY'S GOING TO BE TROUBLE ...

OH... I'VE NEVER BEEN IN THE RECEPTION ROOM BEFORE.
SURU
TSUNA, WAIT!
HUH?
ONE.
WHACK
CRASH

YOU'RE GOIN' DOWN!
I'LL KILL YOU!
WHOOSH
TWO.
FOOSH
!
VOOP
VOOP
WHY YOU ...!
KA-PINK
VO
VO
VO
VOOM
BWAP

ARE YOU INJURED?
YOU'RE PROTECT-ING YOUR RIGHT ARM.
!
THWACK
LOOKS LIKE I'M RIGHT.
CRASH
THREE.
UHH ...
OOOW ...
!

G... GOKUDERA!
YAMAMOTO!
WH... WHY?!
THEY WON'T GET UP.
I MADE SURE OF THAT FOR THOSE TWO.
HUH ?!

DOES THAT MEAN ...
THIS GUY BEAT BOTH OF THEM BY HIMSELF...?!

TAKE YOUR TIME.
I'LL CALL AN AMBULANCE FOR YOU.

WAIT ...
THEN ...

HUH ?!
THIS IS TERRIBLE!

BUT WHY?
WHY DID THIS HAPPEN?
ALL WE DID WAS COME TO THE RECEPTION ROOM...!
!

SQUEAK SQUEAK
WHAT THE ?!

DIE.
BA
SH FFL
RROOAAR
RIP
I WILL DEFEAT YOU WITH DEATHPER-ATION!
WHAT'S WITH THAT?
SOME KIND OF JOKE?
WHA
CK

THUD
DID I BREAK HIS JAW?
WELL, I'D BETTER POUND ON THE OTHER TWO SO THAT...
G... GU...
...THE AMBULANCE WILL TAKE THEM AWAY, TOO.
HUH?
NOT QUITE YET!
BAM

HOP
PLOP
SN
AP
FOOL!
WH
A
P
STAGGER
...
STAGGER
IS IT OKAY ...
BLINK
IF I KILL YOU?

THAT'S ENOUGH.
I DON'T KNOW WHO YOU ARE, LITTLE BOY,
BUT I'M IN A BAD MOOD RIGHT NOW.
MIND LYING DOWN AND WAITING FOR ME?
VO VO
VOOP
YOU ARE STRONG.
CLING
WHOA.
AWESOME, LITTLE BOY.

BAM
THE PARTY'S OVER.
FSH FSH FSH
BOOM
!!

WHAT ?!
YOU ARRANGED THAT ON PURPOSE ?!
IT WAS A RISKY GAMBLE, THOUGH.
YOU WERE LUCKY TO GET OFF WITH JUST BRUISES AND SCRAPES.
SIGH.
WHAT'S THAT SUPPOSED TO MEAN?

Volume 2 - The End

Yawn
PRE

Vision Test
OH BROTHER ...
A VISION TEST.
I CAN'T SEE.
IT'S PITCH BLACK.
BA BANG BANG BANG
CALM DOWN, DOCTOR.

Slaying the Ogres
HIBARI SET OUT TO SLAY THE OGRES.
JAPAN'S BEST
PRE
A DOG JOINED HIM.
I HATE GROUPS.
WHIMPER
A PHEASANT AND A MONKEY TRIED TO JOIN HIM.
I'M GONNA TAKE YOU DOWN.
HYII
HYII
THAT WAS HOW HIBARI BECAME THE BOSS OF OGRE ISLAND.
OH YEAH
THAT'S JUST WRONG!

DID YOU ENJOY THIS BOOK?
SEND IN YOUR LETTERS AND FAN ART!
BLACK AND WHITE ONLY, PLEASE! DO NOT
USE A PENCIL! AND DON'T FORGET TO
INCLUDE YOUR NAME OR PSEUDONYM!

MAIL THEM TO:

REBORN! READERS' HIDEOUT
C/O SHONEN JUMP ADVANCED
VIZ MEDIA, LLC
P.O. BOX 77010
SAN FRANCISCO, CA 94107

Editor-in-charge

HE CAN TALK FOR FIVE HOURS ABOUT HIS HOBBY AND FORGET TO BRING BACK THE MANUSCRIPT AND HE JUST HAD HIS WISDOM TEETH PULLED, BUT HE WORKS VERY HARD. HIS WIFE IS THE CHAMP ON TV'S "TV CHAMPION."

SOUICHI AIDA

Staff and Their Pets

SAKAKI AND UMAKO

KOZATO TAI AND HER BUTLER, SEBASTIAN

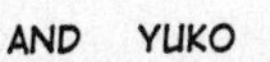

CHRISTINA K. AND YUKO

Clare learns the organization's dark secret...
ALL BOOKS
$7.99!
Claymore
CLAYMORE
6
Vol. 6
On sale Feb. 6!
Claymore
CLAYMORE
1
クレイモア
Claymore™

IN THE NEXT VOLUME...

Tsuna meets I-Ping, a strange child from Hong Kong with incredible martial arts powers. But when Tsuna discovers that I-Ping is an assassin sent to kill him, things start to really get crazy as I-Ping ends up giving Haru and Kyoko poison gyoza buns! There *is* an antidote, but only a single dose—who will Tsuna save, Haru or Kyoko?!

AVAILABLE APRIL 2007!

D.Gray-man™

Vol. 4
On sale Feb. 6!

Allen begins to probe the "Clan of Noah" mystery—the very reason he became an exorcist!

SHONEN JUMP ADVANCED